Wealth Confident

7 Powerful Principles of Godly Success

Identity • Mission • Permission
Excellence • Strategy • Words • Prayer

Elizabeth Brickman

Praise *for* Wealth Confident

"Elizabeth winsomely writes about matters that are close to the heart and inexplicably entwined—money, identity, success. As Christians, she gives us permission to consider these seemingly unholy topics and link them to the very core of our faith in Jesus Christ. Her writing is both an inspiration and an invitation to live a life of uncompromised spiritual joy."

– **Laurie Farquhar**, President, National Christian Foundation, South Florida

"The world is a better place because of Elizabeth Brickman. What a heart! Her ability to bring faith and finance together in practical and spiritual ways is a gift!"

– **Bob Doll**, CEO/CIO, Crossmark Global Investments

"I respect Elizabeth Brickman for her knowledge, her heart, and her focus on encouraging people to have a stronger, happier relationship with God and with money. Elizabeth exemplifies servant-leadership."

– **Ginger Martin**, President & CEO, American National Bank, Broward County's oldest and largest community bank, and Federal Reserve Bank of Atlanta, Miami Branch Board of Directors

"Elizabeth lives and loves generously, and it's contagious. Take some time to encounter the wisdom of this incredible person, and you, too, will grow more generous."

– **Stephan Tchividjian**, CEO & Founder, National Christian Foundation, South Florida

"The world is lucky that they will receive what we received as Elizabeth's clients for over twenty years—Christian and inspiring financial insights and encouragement."

– **Darrell Gwynn**, NHRA Hall of Fame drag racer, Top 50 Drivers of all Time

"Elizabeth Brickman has been a trusted VOICE in the Christian Community on finances for decades. This book is going to have an impact on people my age and for many generations to come."

– **Dr. Bob Barnes**, CEO, Sheridan House Family Ministries, Co-Host, Parenting on Purpose Podcast, and Author

"Spend any time with Elizabeth Brickman, and you will walk away inspired and empowered. God has entrusted rich insight to her, which saturates her coaching, podcasts and writings. Those who share a faith community with Elizabeth know why this winsome wisdom is so effortlessly dispensed. It flows from a deep reservoir of faith in God's timeless truths."

– **Dr. Robey Barnes**, Lead Pastor, City Rev Church

Wealth-Confident: 7 Powerful Principles of Godly Success

End Game Press books may be purchased in bulk at special discounts for sales promotion, corporate gifts, ministry, fund-raising, or educational purposes. Special editions can also be created to specifications. For details, contact Special Sales Dept., End Game Press, P.O. Box 206, Nesbit, MS 38651 or info@endgamepress.com.
Visit our website at www.endgamepress.com.

Library of Congress Control Number:
ISBN: 978-1-63797-266-3
eBook ISBN: 978-1-63797-253-3

Cover design by: Dan Pitts
Interior by Monica Thomas for TLC Book Design, TLCBookDesign.com

Photo Credit Pg. 83 US Airways Flight 1549 author: Greg Li (https://www.flickr.com/photos/22608787@N00) Chesley Sullenberger author: Gage Skidmore (https://www.flickr.com/people/22007612@N05), CC BY-SA 2.0, via Wikimedia Commons

Photo Credit pg. 157 Estate of Stanley Tretick/Corbis Premium Historical via Getty Images

Printed in the United States of America
10 9 8 7 6 5 4 3 2 1

Wealth Confident *is dedicated to my beloved husband, Guy Brickman.*
How did you attain your top 1% status among 19,000 State Farm agents?
... and maintain that high standing for over fifty years?
I asked you how an ordinary person achieves such extraordinary results?
You had no explanation, but I needed to know.

For twenty years, I studied your success-producing, confidence-generating, relationship-building behavior. I dissected every pattern of your attitude and approach. I quantified each of your responses and reactions. I finally figured it out. Your success models seven ancient truths embedded in God's Word.
What a discovery! Now I see how anyone can achieve success.
I hope you won't mind if I share your seven secrets with the world.

For the Lord will be
your confidence,
firm and strong…

PROVERBS 3:26a, AMP

TABLE *of* CONTENTS

Chapter One

FIND YOUR POWER. TRANSFORM YOUR LIFE.

A generous father gave a one-hundred-thousand-dollar gift to each of his adult children. All eight siblings in this family were good-hearted and intelligent, brimming with worthy desires and goals, and thrilled with their windfall. But even this generous sum of money wasn't enough to make dreams come true for seven of them. Each lacked a distinct power necessary for confident financial success.

See if you can find yourself in any of these scenarios. Discover the missing link in your efforts to make life better. When you find your power, you'll transform your life.

Jake and James

Jake was a dear soul who hid a tender secret—he felt unwanted by God. After a few youthful mistakes, he no longer believed he was worthy of God's investment. So he carved a small, careful life, kept a low profile, ignored his talents, and did not ask for or receive much from life.

James had a sunny disposition—but no purpose. He had many good ideas but could never decide which one to pursue. He awakened each day surprised to realize that nothing in his life had changed.

Amy and Ava

Amy was a people-pleaser who served everyone's agenda—except her own. She faithfully devoted every resource to helping build the dreams of others while her own God-inspired dreams languished.

Ava was gifted with the temperament and skills ideally suited to self-employment, but she lacked discipline. If not in the right mood, she couldn't force herself to make the sales call, complete the follow-up, or perform any task she deemed boring.

Zack and Zoe

Zack had a fantastic business idea and knew exactly what he wanted, but he lacked an action plan. Though he greatly appreciated his dad's unexpected cash infusion, it only added to his chaos and confusion. He made hasty decisions, and the money became a wasted opportunity.

Zoe had a rare talent but couldn't control her tongue. Her uncanny ability to pinpoint a client's problem and offer a solution was utterly lost in the wreckage of damaged client relationships caused by her careless words.

Vince and Victoria

Vince was a meticulous planner, but he sought counsel from the wrong places. He looked to celebrities and questionable others to show him the path to success. They misled and used him.

But at last was Victoria, radiant and ready, whose life surged with power and promise.

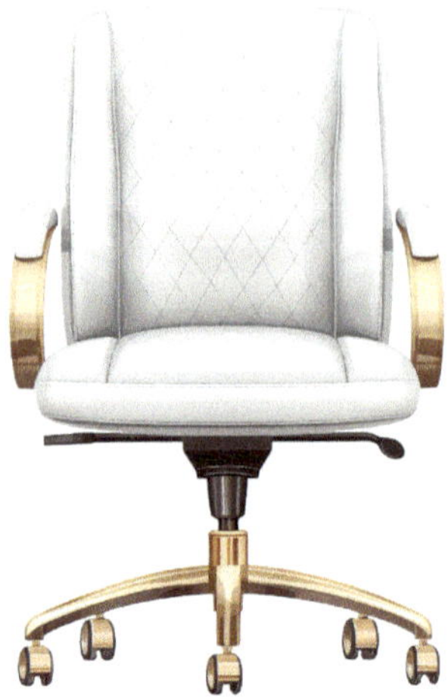

The Power of Seven empowered Victoria to bloom *professionally, relationally,* and *financially* far beyond expectations. These days, she's mobilizing her success to actively invest in Kingdom ministry projects. She hasn't yet arrived at her financial finish line, but she's capable, confident, and committed to creating a lifestyle of radical generosity. When her dad handed her his $100,000 check, she thanked him heartily. Then, she promptly gave half away by opening a donor-advised fund, from which she'll support a variety of ministries over time. Her father's investment in Victoria not only enriched her life but also enriched her chance to make a Kingdom impact.

What sets Victoria apart?

The answer is simple—yet profound.

She understands the precious value of her life in Christ.

She defines each mission she'll take on next.

She permits herself to wholeheartedly commit.

She backs each dream with excellence and discipline.

She details, defines, and executes her strategy.

She uses words wisely.

She prays faithfully and listens intently.

The Power of Seven changed Victoria's life. And it will change yours. This book is for Christians with a drive to succeed—God's way. If you apply these foundational principles to your dreams and goals, they'll equip and prepare you with the financial confidence to succeed.

The Power of Seven is not my invention. Years ago, a colleague of mine named Guy was achieving extraordinary results in his business—and was far more relaxed, confident, and happier than I was in mine. I wondered...what did he know that I'd missed? I dissected every element of his godly approach. I studied every pattern of his success-producing, confidence-generating, relationship-building behaviors. Over time, I realized his attitudes and actions reflected a biblically wise, clarifying expression of God's ancient truths embedded throughout God's word.

I organized these truths into seven distinct power principles that prepare us—richly, from within—to reach our financial potential without losing our way in Christ. They ground us in godly principles and teach us how to succeed—the right way.

We can rely on these truths to help us banish financial insecurity, clarify our thinking, overcome financial obstacles, release our talent, and achieve our purpose.

And because these wealth-confident principles are found throughout God's word, we can trust Him to help us develop them.

Is Wealth Confidence Sinful?

Does God permit us to be wealth-confident? Yes. Why do I believe He wants us to cultivate financial confidence? Because He filled Scripture with over 2,000 references to money. As we adopt His principles, He equips us to manage more—*maybe much more*—for our provision and His glory.

Money is relentless in seeking a higher status in our lives. Still, God wants us to master this unruly tool—owned solely by Him—not by loving it, hating it, or obsessing over it, but by focusing intently on His higher purpose for money.

What Is Wealth Confidence?

Wealth confidence is not arrogance, haughtiness, or greed. The financially confident person does not regard success as some personal payoff arising from their genius or intended for their glory. Rather, it's a way of managing our big, ordained life for the glory of God.

Wealth confidence is:

- Living with a sense of wonder at the utter completeness of God's word as He lays before us His plan for our lives.
- Enlarging our capacity to seize and steward thrilling opportunities.
- Making a substantial Kingdom impact wherever God places us.

"For it is [not your strength, but it is] God who is effectively at work in you, both to will and to work [that is, strengthening, energizing, and creating in you the longing and the ability to fulfill your purpose] for His good pleasure" (Philippians 2:13, AMP).

As you may have gleaned, these powerful principles of wealth confidence are:

1. Identity
2. Mission
3. Permission
4. Excellence
5. Strategy
6. Words
7. Prayer

Let's examine how the Power of Seven set Victoria apart from her siblings and set her up to live a confident, productive life.

The Power of Identity

Victoria has a rock-solid understanding of who she is in Christ.

If we don't know who we are, others will gladly define us. If they define us, they'll control us. God did not make us to be puppets. Or doormats. We must learn to see ourselves through the only eyes that matter—His.

We must learn to see ourselves through the only eyes that matter—His.

The Power of Mission

Victoria knows she is created in Christ Jesus to do good works, prepared in advance for her. So she deliberates prayerfully over what she'll tackle next. She pursues each goal with clarity about her specific objectives.

If we don't choose what we will do, others will choose our path, career, route, and ultimately, our destiny. God does not want us to conform to the paths or plans of others, however well-meaning they may be. We are the ones who must prayerfully define and align our unique purpose.

The Power of Permission

Victoria is never dubious or double-minded after accepting a challenge. Her commitment never wavers when the going gets tough. She doesn't fear failure—or success. She knows God is with her and will use every outcome for His glory.

If we don't give ourselves permission, we'll be double-minded dreamers—not actionable doers. Inner conflict will freeze our dreams into inaction, keeping us from ever moving forward.

The Power of Excellence

Victoria approaches every task impeccably, infusing her profile, profit, and prospects with a standout advantage. Excellence isn't being *the* best, only being *her* best. By highly practiced discipline, she's built her reputation and opened opportunities. She knows the surest way to protect her *yes* is to guard her *no.*

Mediocrity is a low-wattage, low-results way to live. It is powerless to promote confidence or success. Excellence is a magnet that invites opportunity and melts resistance.

The Power of Strategy

Victoria charts her path with a calm, forward-focused mindset as she out-thinks, out-plans, and outwits challenges, always focusing on tomorrow—never yesterday.

If we don't strategize, we make it possible for those without concern for God's mission to out-plan, outwit, and, ultimately, outlast us. God does not want us to charge into battle unprepared and undefended. Like Nehemiah, who examined the ruins of Jerusalem and strategized a plan for rebuilding, we must carefully design and continually adjust a practical path to victory and profit.

The Power of Words

Victoria places guardrails around her tongue in moments of anger or frustration. She speaks hopefully and positively, using her words wisely—to others and to herself. She trades negative self-talk for God-talk.

If we don't learn to bridle our tongues, we put our relationships at risk. A thoughtless word spoken in anger can reverberate through a family or a business for decades. The careless—or targeted—words of friends or foes can penetrate and disempower our greatest efforts.

The Power of Prayer

Victoria prays for God's guidance and His will in every circumstance. She trusts God is who He says He is.

Like Victoria, if we don't constantly communicate with Him in prayer, we untether ourselves from His guidance and influence. To achieve our goals, we need His brilliant, hour-by-hour direction. We are not meant to go it alone.

Victoria is an imperfect, ordinary person, just like you and me. The Power of Seven has equipped her to offer her best to the world around her. She's learned to think, grow, pursue, defend, and steward every resource and build a life of godly success. They've empowered her to upgrade her life into one of confidence and elegance—and they'll upgrade your life too.

Wealth Confident will help you fulfill your ordained accomplishments and build your most effective future. Stretch yourself and reach high to touch the dream of success God has ordained for you. Whatever that dream may be, it will likely require you to manage God's money, an ever-present trigger of stress, yearning, and temptation for us all. *Wealth Confident* concepts are worth learning because well-managed sums of money can do great good for the Kingdom of God!

The chapters ahead will give you a concise track on which to run. They are organized to be an easy diagnostic tool when you struggle. Whether you're starting up, starting over, or finishing well, *Wealth Confident* offers a step-by-step guide to building a strong financial life that will satisfy you—*and glorify God.*

Chapter Two

THE PRINCIPLE OF IDENTITY: Know your God-worth

When dreamers pursue success, they usually start with a strategy. Big mistake. Strategy comes later. Identity must come first.

Identity is the cornerstone of all productivity. It sets off a chain reaction, either toward achievement or failure—in business, finance, relationships, and all of life. That's why it's the first of the seven power principles. Every advance we make—professional, relational, missional, or financial—proceeds from the central truth we believe about who we are.

As Christians, let's bask for a moment in our extreme identity advantage. Ours is wrapped snug in the unsurpassed power of Jesus Christ, in whose name we find hope and promise for the future. Through Him, we can exude the confidence of knowing we are forgiven, healed, established, loved, and called to this earth for a wonderful purpose.

"For the Lord shall be your confidence, firm and *strong..."* (Proverbs 3:26a, AMPC). Our confidence is not in ourselves but in Him. We don't seek worldly self-esteem to bloat the self-life, but rather, a confident identity in Him to strengthen the God-life.

Identity lays a foundation that underwrites our financial success. It's a launchpad for every action you take and every goal you seek. If you get this first power principle right, you're far more likely to get many other life decisions right—at times when you're paying attention—and, more importantly, at times when you are not. Your convictions about who you are determine which opportunities you pursue, avoid, *or even notice.* Identity is the singular root from which every pursuit flows.

Those seemingly "fortunate" Christians we all admire, who reach their dreams with remarkable resiliency and manage to attain success even after overcoming crushing setbacks, are generally those whose identity is solid and sure. Identity is a most precious possession to safeguard, nurture, and protect, no matter what else you lose in life.

So now, it's time to meet a very powerful person: you.

Sacred Gift from God

Your identity is a sacred gift from God, created *by* Him, *for* Him, to serve *His* purposes in the body of Christ. Your life is ordained for you alone. No one else has—or ever will have—the privilege to be you. Therefore, it is safe—*and sacred*—to grow confident in who God made you to be.

Your life is ordained for you alone. No one else has—or ever will have—the privilege to be you.

This is in no way about exalting self-worth but humbly understanding the awesome value of your

God-worth. Through Christ, we can see ourselves through His perfect eyes as a much-loved and worthy child of God.

Your life, with all its pluses and minuses, reflects a highly intentional appointment by a loving God. You serve at the pleasure of the King as a one-of-a-kind, irreplaceable addition to His very big world around us.

Your identity is filled with roaring power. Why? Because its purpose is holy.

The Wonderful Truth About You

Your conception may have been accidental, your past marred by tragedy or injustice, but your *life* is no accident. Your arrival here on earth was ordained. You were created on purpose for a purpose.

As you rested in your mother's womb, the Lord was with you. He formed you, watched you, and appointed all the days of your life before one of them came to be.

Then arrived that great day. Your birth was a *sacred* event, decreed by the Father and celebrated by angels. As seen from Heaven's perspective, the day of your birth was a very big deal.

Examine what Psalm 139 says about your identity so you can live the rest of your days confident in His untarnished dream for you. God, our great orchestrator of good, created you for His pleasure and glory.

"For you created my inmost being; you knit me together in my mother's womb. I praise you because I am fearfully and wonderfully made; your works are wonderful, I know that full well. My frame was not hidden from you when I was made in the secret place, when I was woven together in the depths of the earth. Your eyes saw my unformed body; all the days ordained for me were written in your book before one of them came to be," (Psalm 139:13-16).

Made in Heaven. Sent from Heaven. That's a fact—God's fact—about you.

For a fortunate few, the trusting and confident identity we felt as babies stays locked in place and secure throughout our lives. But for most of us, identity is a malleable substance that swells or shrinks based *not* on God's divine view of us but on external circumstances over which we have little or no control. This should not be.

Let Christ be your confidence. Find and address any area of self-doubt holding you back from pursuing your best life in Him. A weak identity diminishes us and also poses significant risks to our financial future. A confident identity wears like an invisible shield against which hurtful arrows bounce away so we can wake up each day with fresh confidence intact to start anew. Confidence installs a safety valve against worldly temptations and serves as a much-needed buffer against rejections we'll inevitably face, especially when trying to break new ground and push past limits to achieve great goals.

Your Identity Is at Risk

From the moment we are born, our sense of identity is at risk of being marred or stolen. We have an adversary whose mission is no secret. Jesus warned, *"The thief comes only to steal and kill and destroy…"* (John 10:10a). A confident identity is a tantalizing target for the evil one.

The thief is hell-bound to *steal* our identity in Christ, *kill* our confidence, and *destroy* our efforts to create full, successful, and rewarding lives. Make no mistake. Satan is out to harm you.

And it's not just him. Throughout your lifetime, people and circumstances have likely influenced your identity in ways neither you nor they comprehend. From the nasty kid on the playground to the teacher who gave you a failing grade, the sibling who said hurtful things, the employer who didn't think you were worthy of promotion, the prospect who said no to you but yes to another, the friend who betrayed you, the beloved one who chose someone else...there are endless identity influencers that cause us harm and damage.

All it takes is a careless gesture or unkind word to have a profound lifetime effect. One small incident, a single disappointment, may poke holes in your confidence and foster a gnawing sense of inadequacy that lasts for years.

We mourn the talent that fell short of the prize, the submission that fell short of acceptance, the looks that fell short of the beauty contest, the score that fell short of the win, or the relationship that fell short of the engagement ring.

Sometimes, our identity is destroyed through a single trauma.

Emma's Story

When Emma was a little girl, her family was involved in a public scandal. They had to leave town abruptly and start a new life elsewhere, leaving everything behind.

Emma's identity was destroyed, and she was filled with a shame she could not understand.

The grown-ups couldn't help her—because they didn't know. A confident identity lives inside, unseen, but identity's ramifications reverberate powerfully across a life, a family, a career, a marriage, and often span generations.

Over time, Emma assembled a patchwork new identity for herself in the worst possible way, from the outside in, absorbing faulty clues about who she was from others around her.

Who did she allow to define her identity? Anyone. Everyone. Teachers. Bullies. The cold-hearted. The mean-spirited. She had no ability to discern who should or should not impact her confidence because young Emma could not yet know the wonderful woman God had created her to be.

People-pleasing became her life raft—a dangerous mindset, especially for a child. The strangers who entered her new life could only peer at her through a cloudy lens of external circumstances. They didn't know the real Emma. By the time she stumbled into adulthood, she didn't know the real Emma, either.

How will we manage to do all the wonderful things He created us to do if we don't even know the wonderful person He created us to *be*?

It's not the occurrences outside us but the beliefs within us, about us, that drive us toward our eventual life outcomes, be they spectacular or dismal. Faithful and devoted to God though you may be, a flawed identity will suppress your future, no matter how valiantly you try to make life work. You need a secure and fortified identity in Christ so you may be victorious as you battle real-life disappointments, enemy assaults from hell, or the late-night musings of an insecure mind.

What is the basis of your identity? It's important that you know. Do you see yourself through the lens of your personal and family history? Or through the lens of God's ordained plan for your life?

In adulthood, Emma became a Christian, a devoted Jesus follower. But until she realized her identity needed to disconnect from her past and root itself in the deep love of Christ, her old, damaged identity cost her countless opportunities to live the abundant life Jesus wants for us all. Mistakes happened. Unwise choices were made—not because she was so sinful—but because she was so scared. And so rooted in a damaged identity.

From a damaged identity…

- You'll think you have a need you do not have.
- You'll be blind to a need you actually do have.
- You'll over-strategize issues never intended for you.
- You'll work to be someone God never made you to be at all.
- You'll bypass blessings and fail to activate dreams that were yours to fulfill.
- You'll miss the achievements God appointed you to attain.

Until you step purposefully into your true identity as a child of the King of Kings, you'll be unnecessarily unsure, anxiously measuring your skewed sense of smallness against the seeming bigness of everyone else around you in business, finance, relationships, marriage, and life.

No matter your history, you must not allow anyone to define you except the Lord. You are not who *they* say you are, who *they* think you are, or who *they* insist you become. You are who God says you are—God and no one else.

Let's agree to dump the untruths about our inadequacy once and for all. Of course, we are inadequate! That's why Jesus died—to save us from our inadequate selves. Jesus died so we would not have to be perfect because we cannot be perfect, no matter how hard we try.

Do you fear you are not enough? If Jesus lives within you, you are enough because He is enough. Period.

Reverse the Curse

Over time, God showed Emma how to reverse the identity curse in her life. Against all odds, He allowed her to achieve high goals and fulfill big dreams. She moved past childhood sorrow onto lasting grown-up love and exceptional business success. Look what God can do—for Emma *and for you.*

The world is under the deception and oppression of the enemy of your soul and mine. Let's take back what God Himself ordained for us and what Jesus made possible for us: a confident identity in Him.

Know your God-worth. Cherish it. The world tries to twist and contort it. The world wants to *conform you* to its culture. God wants to *transform you* by changing your mind. *"Do not conform to the pattern of this world, but be transformed by the renewing of your mind. Then you will be able to test and approve what God's will is—his good, pleasing and perfect will,"* (Romans 12:2).

Start today to live in the power of your identity. Let the truth of who you are in Christ fortify you to withstand any battle, delay, or setback on your path to God-inspired success. A relaxed and confident identity in Christ will open ordained doors for you—personally, professionally, financially, and relationally—by extinguishing the fear and self-doubt that have held you back, limited your progress, and kept you stuck.

Your life is *on purpose*—for *God's* purpose. When you see yourself differently, you'll change the outcome of everything.

For personal reflection and discussion:

1. What circumstances or persons have most swayed your identity from its true center?
2. In what way have you limited yourself personally, professionally, financially, or relationally, based on a false idea of who you are?
3. By employing your Christ-confident identity as an invisible shield, what dream will you find the courage to pursue next?

Chapter Three

AUTHENTICITY:
The End of Pretend

One fascinating part of God's plan was to create you with a unique identity all your own. Your authentic identity is a sacred gift from God given to you alone and to no other. No one else has the privilege to be you. This is not a statement of arrogance but of reverence for the God who chose to knit you together in the womb to fulfill His plan, not yours.

Living in insistent authenticity is how you honor His gift of the unique life entrusted to you, with faith and humility. You tremble with awe that He chose you to perform *His* work throughout *His* land.

As Christians, authenticity is our posture of reverence and gratitude.

As Christians, authenticity is our posture of reverence and gratitude.

In the past, you may have been afraid to live life authentically or to reveal your authentic self to those around you. Your relational and professional fears are justifiable. We all want to fit in, but living in your authentic personality, style, and identity—the one God Himself chose for you—is your safest spot in the universe. It's the place where

God wants you to reside. It's a way for you to navigate through life powerfully and joyfully as a representative of Jesus and to fulfill those specific works He's assigned to you alone. Remember, before you chose Him, He chose you—to do wonderful things through Him and for Him.

God's Protection

Authenticity is neither self-inflation nor humanistic defiance, but rather God's protection, a safeguard to keep you on His ordained path by removing the confusion of other people's standards over your career, income, wealth, spending, and lifestyle. When you're deeply committed to living authentically, you discern more clearly those holy pursuits you were born and gifted to accomplish, and you're quicker to graciously discard those dreams never intended for you. You'll feel confident saying no to those "not-intended-for you" pursuits.

You are God's one and only you, made in Heaven, sent to earth to fulfill His plan. In order to do what He created you to do (see Psalm 139:16), you must trust who He created you to be.

No More Pretending

My dear client, Carl, was a dentist—the sweetest, saddest dentist I'd ever encountered. Since childhood, he'd been fascinated with world history, and he'd always dreamed of becoming a history professor. But his well-meaning family pushed him to follow the medical path.

Compliant Carl spent years pursuing a mission he never wanted. He lived dutifully—and sorrowfully. It took everything he had to force himself to work each day. As his practice grew, his heart shrank. He felt trapped. Carl loved the Lord, and he loved people, but for him, success was but a hollow shell.

That's the heartbreak of inauthentic achievement. After you attain it, you face the worst kind of despair.

I felt a tender sadness whenever I met with Carl. I'm thankful for his trust in revealing his secret heartache to me. Mercifully, God opened a path for faithful Carl to exit his practice early. I couldn't help but wonder what his life might have been like had he pursued his true dream. Surprisingly, although physicians tend to earn more than professors, his financial result would have been about equal because he'd have tried harder and worked longer if he could only have worked in the field he truly loved.

"And do not be conformed to this world [any longer with its superficial values and customs], but be transformed and *progressively changed [as you mature spiritually] by the renewing of your mind [focusing on godly values and ethical attitudes], so that you may prove [for yourselves] what the will of God is, that which is good and acceptable and perfect [in His plan and purpose for you],"* (Romans 12:2, AMP). By living authentically, you'll safeguard your dreams of relational, financial, and professional success.

The authentic Christian realizes that living someone else's life or fulfilling someone else's destiny is not authentic living. That's pretending. What reward lies at the end of pretend? Emptiness. If we do not embrace the person God made us to be and the dream He's planted in our hearts, we throw into the trash bin that which is sacred and intended for sacred purpose.

This does not suggest we pause from work until our dream job shows up. Far from it. Over the course of our lifetimes and careers, especially in early adulthood or when starting out or starting over, we'll often have to accept jobs that don't mesh in the slightest with our talents or inclinations. Sometimes, God blatantly places us where we don't want to be. At those stressful times, we say a trusting *yes* to the Lord and prayerfully await His next move.

I am one of countless Christ followers who had to surrender a career I loved to a career I dreaded. Later, He miraculously rerouted me to the career of my dreams—and His. I was astonished to realize there would have been no other way to get me there. My situation is not unique. God's doorways are invisible until we obediently walk through them. Only then do we see the light on the other side. But as much as it depends on us, let's not pursue any path without committing to authenticity.

The Financial Advantage of Authenticity

Living authentically gives you an undeniable financial advantage. It's a brilliant way to make money. No matter what product or service a competitor offers, the one and only product they cannot offer or duplicate is...*you.*

Think of those who've attained great success in business, sports, or entertainment. Have you noticed the obvious common denominator? There's always something *just a little different* about successful people. They stand out among their peers.

Everybody laughed when a young Dolly Parton announced her goal to be a worldwide superstar. But this country girl was just different enough to be memorable. Had she tried to fit in with all the other young, blonde Hollywood celebrities of her time, would we even remember her name? Doubtful. The success potential of living in your authentic style is unlimited.

And it's not just celebrities who enjoy an advantage. Here are a few examples of authentic success among people I have known:

- Refined Robert's manners are impeccable. He's a bit more formal than most in his dress code and style, at the table and even in the car. It's just who he authentically is. His clients enjoy his personal brand of cordial formality, and they send him all the business he can handle. His company has grown extremely large. His advertising budget is zero.
- Red-headed RoseAnn's conversations are interspersed with exuberant words in Italian. Almost no one understands her—but everyone adores her. Her heritage is Irish, not Italian, but Italy is her personal brand. Her South Florida home has all the ambiance of a Tuscan villa. Everyone wants to be near her and do business with her.

Why try to fit in if God has given you a thrilling chance to stand out? Be thankful if you look, sound, or *just are* a little different. No copying others anymore. Why discard your unique financial advantage?

Embracing authenticity does not limit you. It keeps the marketplace from diluting you.

Embracing authenticity does not limit you. It keeps the marketplace from diluting you. That's a fact.

Should I Deny Self?

Jesus said that whoever wants to be His disciple must deny themselves, take up their cross daily, and follow Him (Matthew 16:24). Denying self doesn't mean denying who God made us to be. It means rejecting the willful, sinful, culture-embracing, God-separating self that God did *not* make us to be—and putting everything, including popularity and profit, underneath the supreme lordship of Christ.

As Christians, we don't need to fit in. We need to stand out.

Let's fiercely resist becoming the person who...

> ...Our culture expects us to be.
>
> ...Our past ensnares us to be.
>
> ...Our stockholders demand us to be.
>
> ...Our toxic relationships harass us to be.
>
> ...The enemy of our soul lures us to be.

Why My Quirky Identity?

Why did God assign you a unique identity? To support the body of Christ. You've been formed and fashioned just right for the special assignments God has for you.

You, dear one, offer exactly what a certain someone needs *from God.* You are His delivery system, His boots on the ground, custom-made to deliver precisely what is missing...in a business, culture, community, or family. Yes, it turns out, the person delivering the missing ministerial ingredient is...*you*!

Once you stop trying to imitate others around you, God's power will be unleashed through you. His Kingdom expands not despite our differences but *because* of them.

"God has given each of you some special abilities; be sure to use them to help each other, passing on to others God's many kinds of blessings," (1 Peter 4:10, TLB). If God has made you as one who looks or sounds a little different from others, He did so on purpose.

Can you handle this truth?

You should *revel* in this truth.

Reclaiming Authenticity

Pop quiz: Are you authentic? Or inauthentic? You probably don't even know.

Most of us are unconsciously inauthentic. Our manner, style, and personalities have been composed of elements grabbed at moments when we needed to survive—in the playground, classroom, boardroom, or marketplace. Or when we've hastily fabricated people-pleasing responses in a feeble attempt to make peace, gain popularity, or not be left behind.

Over time, our personalities become composites of an ongoing "snatch and grab" operation as we've patched together our personal style. It has functioned as our coping mechanism to get by, get past, or get ahead.

If our childhood was marked by trauma or abuse, inauthenticity may have been our safety cloak. What began as a survival technique may now be well entrenched. But your authentic personality—the original, untainted one—is a God-fashioned act of sacred creation. He formed you according to His blueprint—not other people's.

Remember, before you chose Him, He chose you—to do wonderful things for His Kingdom. God has an exciting plan to bless others through you. Living authentically will give you the best chance to fulfill your holy destiny.

Authenticity in the Body of Christ

Until you adopt authenticity as your personal brand, you'll be racked by a false sense of inadequacy, protesting that you weren't given the talent, skill, or opportunity to be whomever you dreamed of being...before you dreamed of being you.

We are all multi-faceted jewels, given only twenty-four hours a day and one short lifetime. If you waste time jealously yearning to switch talents or abilities with another, if you envy others who are strong in areas where you're weak, you'll use up your lifetime without fulfilling your ordained destiny.

There is a path God designed for you alone. You cannot bequeath it to another. God made you to be *this*, not *that*.

In the past, you may have been enslaved to the approval of others. Let God alone be the stronghold of your life. Seek to conform only to the image of His Son—and not to the image of anyone else.

You need not exhaust yourself striving for perfection. You'll never be perfect, and that's perfectly okay. You have intrinsic worth because you are His prized possession—not because you are perfect, but because you are His.

"Now here is what I am trying to say: All of you together are the one body of Christ, and each one of you is a separate and necessary part of it," (1 Corinthians 12:27, TLB). Each one of us is a separate and necessary part of the body of Christ. We need not emulate the popular or become zombie-like, robotically emptying ourselves of the very differences God says He built into us. Each of us is needed in our own quirky, imperfect, wonderful way.

Christianity is not a club—it's a body. We will succeed, and His Kingdom will grow, not despite our differences but because of them.

The confusion around our identity must decrease, and the voice of God must increase. You are not who people say you are—or want you to become. You are not who your inner voice accuses—or boasts. You are who God says you are—God and no one else. He's imprinted you with a one-of-a-kind identity. Let no one subvert it. God alone is the stronghold of your life. He formed you according to His blueprint—not anyone else's. You've been formed and fashioned just right for the special assignments He has for you.

Ask God to help you shun your former people-pleasing tactics. *"The fear of man brings a snare, but whoever leans on, trusts in,* and *puts his confidence in the Lord is safe* and *set on high,"* (Proverbs 29:25, AMPC). Conform to the image of His Son and no other. Not to the employer above you, the peer beside you, or the popular among you.

When you untwist from the contortions of trying to be all things to all people, you're finally going to have a good time being you!

Hold tightly to your sacred, God-given identity, no matter what the culture coerces or influencers tempt. Grant no one but God the authority to define you. Be who God made you to be—and no other. Reverently honor, steward, and safeguard the unique *life*print that is yours, for you are here on a heavenly mission.

For personal reflection and discussion:

1. Who most shaped your identity? How did they do so?
2. Under what circumstances do you feel tempted to fit in rather than stand out?
3. Describe a time or an event when you felt free to be your truest self. What emotion did you feel toward yourself and toward those around you?

Chapter Four

GODFIDENCE:
Holy Courage To Activate Dreams

Accomplishing any big goal will require an insane amount of confidence. Throughout your successful life, you'll need to stir up new waves of this confidence again and again. You'll need it this time, next time, every time, for every goal, project, pursuit, or enterprise you take on.

And you'll need confidence long before you've earned it. For without confidence, you'll find it impossible to generate the mental stamina and fortitude required to push past your limits.

Confidence is an elusive elixir, a *serum of success.* It's so coveted that if sold by the ounce, it would cost more than gold, for it empowers you to *spin* gold out of ideas and build a fabulous life. But confidence cannot be purchased at any price.

Confidence acts as the jaws of life, extricating you from your comfort zone. Once you're unbound from your stronghold of fear, you become free to pursue the brave new world of success: personal, professional, missional, and financial.

Confidence draws an indelible line between the futures of those who…

…make the call vs. make up a reason to procrastinate.

…step forward in faith vs. bury their talent in the ground.

…knock on opportunity's door vs. stand back for someone else to open it.

The Power of Identity has three components: *knowing, being, and doing.* Chapter 2 was about *knowing* who we are in Christ and how precious and valuable our life is in Him. Chapter 3 was about *being* authentic and true to our uniquely-designed selves.

Confidence is about *doing*—about finding the courage to act rather than just dream. In this final aspect of the Power of Identity, you'll discover how to instantly access confidence on demand so you can push past fears and insecurities. Confidence is not a frivolous extra—it is essential. Ignore it at your own peril.

Can You Reach Your Dreams Without Confidence?

We all know wonderful people who have sabotaged life's best outcomes by self-doubt. We pray for them regularly due to their seeming inability to move ahead with their dreams or plans, whether financial, professional, or personal. It's often the missing piece in their underperformance puzzle. You know who I'm talking about...

...The educated and qualified relative afraid to send a résumé.

...The young adult too nervous to schedule a job interview.

...The perpetually stuck friend who has an innovative idea, perfectly planned, needing no financial outlay, yet finding every reason to stall.

...The brainy child who wants to earn an advanced degree or designation but is immobilized by fear.

You love these people. You inquire with hope about their progress. Sadly, the answer is always the same. The train never leaves the station.

A lack of confidence is a steel trap binding us to today's unfulfilling sameness. Without forward motion, expansion, or fuel to fire up progress, our dream eventually suffocates from a lack of oxygen.

Like it or not, know it or not, want it or not, our financial future—and all the business relationships and strategies that govern it—will be partly driven by our confidence. Without it, you won't seek the promotion, try out for the team, sign up for the class, sit for the exam, send the résumé, or even say hello to the bigwig at the business event.

Carla's Story

Carla was a talented young beauty with a big personality. From kindergarten, the adults were wowed by her innate ability to influence others. Her emotional intelligence was off the charts. Everyone predicted she'd choose a career in public relations—which she did. But despite her giftedness, Carla lacked that elusive elixir of confidence. For reasons no one could figure out, this persuasive charmer, after earning her communications degree, froze with anxiety. She could not even bring herself to submit a résumé.

Though incomprehensible to her family, she chose instead to become a restaurant host—for nearly a decade.

Why Some Succeed

You probably know someone with a bit less talent and ability than you. They may have less skill, exert less effort, or appear to be less committed than you. Yet they're achieving big dreams and developing important relationships faster than you. You can't find any objective reason justifying them to outpace you, yet, against all odds, they are killing it in a way you are not.

Where do they generate the bravery to aim beyond the limits of their present abilities? How do they access the courage to reach for lofty goals while you, who have more talent, drive, or skill, settle for less?

These enviable achievers are pressing hard on an accelerator few Christians understand—holy confidence, the gas pedal for anyone who wants to upgrade their life, accomplish something significant, or live out their highest purpose in Christ.

Guy's Story

Guy was offered an opportunity to open a franchise insurance agency. It was an exciting way to build a business of his own while safely tethered to a large, well-established insurance company offering success systems he could model for his own business.

All new agents were advised to contact ten prospects daily for the first thirty days. They were to inquire when the prospect's current insurance would expire and follow up with a quote right before that date. The company encouraged that contacting three hundred prospective households would, over time, help them establish a good-sized agency of their own.

As new agents, they were understandably shy, nervous, and uncomfortable about calling or visiting strangers. Most imagined every sort of rejection and embarrassment in making dreaded contact with strangers; they surrendered to their fears and never made contact at all. After all, they reasoned, they were in business for themselves now. They were their own bosses.

Guy chose a different approach. He strategized that if he doubled the recommended number of daily contacts from ten to twenty, he might double the size of his agency. If he tripled the project's time period from thirty to ninety days, he might triple his result.

He didn't triple it. He quadrupled it—and quadrupled it again. He built one of the largest franchise insurance agencies in the United States.

Why was it easy for him to finish what others could not bring themselves to start? Confidence. The strength of Guy's Christ-centered identity was strong and secure. The word "no" held no power to upset his mood, his mind, or his day. No rejection ever felt catastrophic or even personal. Rejection had no impact on him whatsoever. He felt he was God's beloved child doing worthy tasks for a worthy goal. He believed in his product—and in his Lord. For him, making new business connections or talking with new prospects was a no-risk endeavor. He thought it was fun.

Decades later, he hosted a political campaign event for a candidate who later became governor. Right before the event, he jotted a note to himself to ask the candidate about life insurance. I was incredulous. "Ask *him?*"

"Why not? He needs to buy it from *somebody,*" said Guy. "Why not me? All he can do is say no."

The Confidence Conundrum

Confidence plays hard to get—and easy to lose. The very pursuit of it is exhausting. The constant setbacks of confidence are infuriating. Just when you think you're getting close, the goal line moves. It's so unfair when the littlest mishap or cutting criticism costs you all the confidence it took months to gain.

Confidence never shows up when you need it most. It's always too late. You need it *before* success arrives—not after. But it rarely blooms until *after* we've proven ourselves, *after* we've signed the client, scored the field goal, or won the industry award.

Worst of all, confidence is spiritually risky business, a dangerous cousin to arrogance, ego, and pride. It can carve a dangerous idol out of self-sufficiency. It's a spiritual tightrope laden with risk.

But there is a secret to holy confidence... Ask God to loan you His.

The Godfidence Solution

"For the Lord shall be your confidence, firm and *strong, and shall keep your foot from being caught [in a trap or some hidden danger],"* (Proverbs 3:26, AMPC). I call this Godfidence—notice big G. Little i. Godfidence is holy courage that empowers you to pursue Heaven-inspired dreams.

Godfidence is always there when you need it. It arrives before you earn it. It never needs to be reinforced by man or mind. And it is 100% endorsed by the Lord.

Godfidence is confidence—minus the hazard of pride. It's not based on the elevation of self—or on self at all—but on God, a perfect Father we can trust to equip us for any challenge.

Godfidence is courage made easy. Courage done right. It's a divine partnership between you and the Father, allowing you to stretch beyond yourself and seek new endeavors, knowing He is your holy safety net to catch you if you fall.

Godfidence is courage without conceit, boldness without brashness, fearlessness without foolishness. As you can see in Scripture, it's the *only* kind of confidence God approves.

How Godfidence Activates High Achievement

Godfidence leashes our esteem to God's hand so we can unleash our focus without fear of failure.

It gives us the courage to stretch beyond our present abilities.

Godfidence merges our imperfections and weaknesses with God's perfection and strength. This holy "merger and acquisition" fuses our incomplete resources with God's perfect sufficiency to complete our tasks.

It provides us with the staying power and resilience to meet and overcome lingering challenges. It's stronger and more enduring than any other type of courage we might master or feebly muster on our own. It conserves our limited energy by refueling us with holy energy from the wellspring that never runs dry.

Godfidence provides inner certainty while pressing toward an uncertain future. It's attitude before outcome—and sometimes, it's attitude despite outcome.

It bypasses the risk of sin. We are safe when we're sure of who we are *in Him.*

In Godfidence, our courage is strengthened and reinforced; our thinking is reframed. We bravely cast off interference, maximize strengths, and harness opportunities without the crippling fear of failure. And the best part is…

We don't have to earn it, learn it, practice it, or marshal the will to sustain it. All it requires is asking the Lord to be our confidence. Ask Him today.

Do you remember the children's story about the little engine that could? That's a perfect example of Godfidence.

As you strive to make life wonderful, let Him be your confidence, for you are God's chosen one, His beloved.

"Blessed [with spiritual security] is the man who believes and *trusts in* and *relies on the* LORD *And whose hope* and *confident expectation is the* LORD. *For he will be [nourished] like a tree planted by the waters, That spreads out its roots by the river; And will not fear the heat when it comes; But its leaves will be green* and *moist. And it will not be anxious* and *concerned in a year of drought Nor stop bearing fruit,"* (Jeremiah 17:7-8, AMP).

The Godfidence Prayer

"Lord, I trust You—not myself. I trust Your love for me, Your plan for me, and Your protection of me. I yield my will to Yours; therefore, in any circumstance that feels like rejection, I can trust that what is disguised as rejection is Your protection over my path. I can activate my dream with holy courage, and I will fear no one, for You, O God, will be my confidence."

For personal reflection and discussion:

1. Do you recall an incident when you lost your confidence due to a mistake? Was it a public or a private error? How did you handle it outwardly? How did you handle it on the inside?
2. Do you know someone who struggles with a lack of confidence? After reading this chapter, what can you now say to that person?
3. What will change for you when approaching your dream or next challenge with Godfidence?

Chapter Five

THE PRINCIPLE OF MISSION:
What Exciting Adventure Is Next?

At some point, we all dared to dream of our future. Ask any five-year-old, "What do you want to be when you grow up?" and you'll hear a happy, confident reply.

"I want to be an astronaut," he lisps through missing teeth.

"I want to be a surgeon," she twinkles, tossing pigtails over her shoulder.

But for some of us, growing up means giving up.

Maybe you feel stuck in the wrong career or trapped on the wrong financial track.

Can your life get unstuck? Yes.

The energizing Power of Mission will help you reclaim the confidence of your youth so you can build what God wants you to build. It's not too hard. And it's not too late.

"For we are God's handiwork, created in Christ Jesus to do good works, which God prepared in advance for us to do," (Ephesians 2:10). Notice that "good works" is plural—we will take on many missions over our lifetime. Even a mission adopted later in life can rescue us from an unfulfilling path of regret because *our* good works are *God's idea.*

God's plan is for His loved ones to spread out, with influence, throughout the earth. He embeds us in a specific sphere of society so we may *do* something...*be* something...or *accomplish* something.

You can be excited to explore your dreams and passions, including vocational, educational, relational, and aspirational goals, and bring your vision into focus. The talents you've been given and the favor you have received are by no means accidental. Your innate abilities are on purpose—for His purpose.

You haven't run out of time to build the exciting life God ordained. Laura Ingalls Wilder began writing *Little House on the Prairie* at age sixty-five; it later became a beloved television series. Colonel Harland Sanders established the Kentucky Fried Chicken restaurant chain also at age sixty-five; nine years and six hundred franchises later, he sold his share for millions.[1] No matter how late you start, you really can finish well.

Running Ahead of God

As a Christian surrendered to Christ, have you ever wondered, *dare I dream at all?*

I believe the answer is an unqualified yes. We would not be alive at this moment if God had not decreed it. And why does He keep us alive? To fulfill His mission for our lives.

1 "Successful Seniors: 10 Stories of Purpose Discovered Later in Life." Friendship. June 25,2021. https://www.friendship.us/insights/successful-seniors.

As Christians, our every dream pulsates with the possibility of holy purpose. Yet, sometimes we're so afraid of running ahead of God that we don't run toward any goal at all.

Why not partner with the One who knows more about your purpose than you do? Why not run alongside Him in faith and trust? As Christians, we bring the light of Christ into every sphere. Nothing we do is about us alone, and no mission is ever about that mission alone.

You may feel "called" to a certain path and wonder if God could be behind it. Isn't it amazing to consider that your dream of success may be His dream, too?

Isn't it amazing to consider that your dream of success may be His dream, too?

Your Dream: What Were You Born to Do?

I'll use myself as an example. I love business, sales, and marketing. I love Jesus *and* I love business. The two may seem incongruous, yet they are not in conflict at all—they are exactly what God needs me to love to motivate me to be in the places He's ordained for my life.

As a woman of *actionable* faith, I dare to dream. I want to celebrate and use my gifts, talents, and opportunities—not waste them. I long to experience the fruit of my labor, not in foolish conceit, but in the kind of godliness God rewards. Ultimately, I want the stewardship of my life to count. I don't want to scatter my life's effort to the wind but to focus and orchestrate a tangible *something*.

I believe that's what you want too. But what does God want?

God's Dream: You Were Born for Productivity

You were born on purpose. Born for a cause.

Your days are ordained. Your work is appointed.

God has dreams for your life, and He has written about those dreams in great detail throughout Scripture. *"For we are His workmanship, [His own master work, a work of art], created in Christ Jesus [reborn from above—spiritually transformed, renewed, ready to be used] for good works, which God prepared [for us] beforehand [taking paths which He set], so that we would walk in them [living the good life which He prearranged and made ready for us],"* (Ephesians 2:10, AMP).

So you can see why it is the will of the Father for us to thrive and succeed in good works—*not for our glory,* but *for His.* Jesus said, *"The thief comes only to steal and kill and destroy; I have come that they may have life, and have it to the full,"* (John 10:10).

This fullness, this abundance, is not about luxury cars and frivolous goodies but about a rock-solid richness—an indestructible reservoir—that abides within you and overflows beyond the borders of your inner self to bless and impact the world around you. Material riches may come—or not. We have no way of knowing God's highest financial will for our lives, but we can do everything in our power not to hinder His best financial plan.

What if you don't know what it is you want to do? Let's consider the heart of all human endeavor.

As a Christian, the overarching purpose of your life and work is crystal clear. Whether you dream of being a stockbroker, yacht broker, minister of music, or prime minister of a country, your core mission and underlying purpose is always the same: to glorify God. No matter your mission, you're *in the ministry.*

Accordingly, you are to meet and encounter certain others within your particular life calling. Don't worry; God will choreograph these circumstances and orchestrate divine connections to position you to achieve His holy plan.

Our lives are on purpose—for God's purpose. Even before you know your mission, you can trust your value.

What Do You Dream of Doing?

What would you like to do with your beautiful life? The possibilities are tantalizing.

Would you like to build a family, a ministry, a unique enterprise? Start a business or earn a graduate degree? Double your revenue, succeed in your career, or maybe trade it in for a new one? Exercise a talent, or attain a credential?

Is your mission to survive the loss of a loved one, invest in a new relationship, or begin a new chapter?

Or maybe your dream is to pause—as in, cease and desist—from your present lifestyle, work, or activities. You want to turn off the noise, carve out some quality time with God, and discern just what it is *He* wants you to do with your life.

The World is a Noisy Place

Until you live in the power of your God-ordained, personal mission, others will choose your path, career, goals, and, ultimately, your destiny. But God does not want you to conform to the plans of others, however well-meaning they may be. *"Do not conform to the pattern of this world, but be transformed by the renewing of your mind. Then you will be able to test and approve what God's will is—his good, pleasing and perfect will,"* (Romans 12:2).

Are you confounded to a standstill by unsolicited and conflicting advice concerning your future?

The world is a rather noisy place, full of opinions and ideas. When pressured with too many choices, sometimes it feels safer to paddle in our own pond and let the waves of "fate" wash over us.

Please don't do that. When you were a child, the adults led. You were helpless to follow. Now, you are an adult. With the Lord at the helm, together, you and He must lead your life.

For a dreamer, inaction *is* action—of the worst kind. The problem with standing still is that nothing else in life stops—except you.

You don't need a pep talk.

You don't need to trade for another person's life.

You need a God-inspired mission of your very own. If you don't define the parameters of how and where to direct your life efforts, others will gladly define them for you. To the extent you allow it, you'll feel empty and powerless. Something inside you knows you were not born to fulfill anybody else's dream for your life except the Lord's.

"Fear of man will prove to be a snare, but whoever trusts in the LORD *is kept safe,"* (Proverbs 29:25). When others define our mission, the fleeting days of our lives are lived by default. Default that is their fault. And your fault. But never God's fault. He has something better for you. So let's figure it out.

16 Questions to Help You Identify Your Mission

Our lives are ordained with gifts, talents, and a purpose of which we may not yet be aware. Even if you have no mission in mind, you've come into this world pre-wired for His service. *"Yet you, LORD, are our Father. We are the clay, you are the potter; we are all the work of your hand,"* (Isaiah 64:8).

Are you flustered by the array of possibilities? Then don't look for a career—look for the ideal way you'd like to relate to the world around you. This will be a sound process for peeling away the layers of complexity and uncovering your best-fitting, God-given path.

Here's a dreaming exercise that has helped some clients clear the cobwebs and open fresh, creative juices. Let it gently lead you…

1. Imagine you are working with other people. In what role? Are you influencing? Selling? Teaching? Guiding? Instructing? Listening? Problem-solving? Healing? Fixing? Caring?
2. Choose one: team or solo work?
3. Are you energized by juggling multiple activities? Or do you prefer to hyper-focus on one thing at a time?
4. Do you prefer noise? Or quiet?
5. Do you prefer to sit? Stand? Or move?
6. Do you like to be indoors or outdoors?
7. Do you like to dress up or dress casually? How do you feel about uniforms, such as a physician, airline captain, or firefighter clothing?
8. How do you feel about travel, airports, and unfamiliar places?

9. Do you prefer continuous client engagement (presumably with long-term customers or clients), or do you enjoy turning strangers into new friends every day?
10. Do you prefer to communicate in person? In writing? Electronically? By phone? Not at all?

11. Do you like to proactively execute planned projects and tasks? Or do you find it more energizing to respond to unplanned requests?
12. What subject is guaranteed to spring new energy into your being every time—even when you have no energy for anything else?
13. What activity makes time stand still? This is especially important because, whatever your mission, you'll have to do "it" again and again and again.
14. Where do you see yourself in your imaginary work scenario? Sitting among others? Behind a desk? Standing? Are there many people around? Is there fresh air? What are you holding in your hands? A tool? A pen? A gavel? Are you instructing? Listening? Solving? Fixing?
15. Name a wrong in this world you wish you could make right. Some of the most passionate missions are born from an intense desire to right a wrong.
16. Perhaps your mission will be God's way of redeeming a sorrow, injustice, or illness that happened to you, by guarding it from happening to another. What might that be?

Step Forward

You may not always know in advance where you're headed or why. But you're beginning to see how God gives us the Power of Mission to fulfill His plan for our lives. That's why we can step confidently into our future, trusting Him to guide and direct us.

Perhaps for no explicable reason, you are magnetized, irresistibly drawn to a particular occupation. And if that career generates financial prosperity, so be it. God owns it all anyway, and *"it is he who gives you the ability to produce wealth,"* (Deuteronomy 8:18).

That, too, is for God's good pleasure and purpose. He'll show you what He wants you to do with the money. Be sure to ask—and obey.

Going forward, you'll continue to define and activate your mission and give shape to your dream. You'll learn how to overcome obstacles and challenges—both external and internal. You'll be empowered to embrace and complete your mission.

But for now…begin to make some faith-filled decisions for your life. Take thoughtful, prayerful steps to clarify your next mission. There may be dozens of missions over your lifetime. You need only focus on the next one.

Stretch your creative muscle and begin to shape and form that fuzzy dream. Begin to plan it, consider it, chart it, pray over it, and count its cost, just like Nehemiah did in the Bible when he led the Israelites to rebuild the Jerusalem wall in fifty-two days.

Decide to step forward without excuse or delay.

Allow your consecrated heart to woo you toward a profession, hobby, or enterprise. Trust the Holy Spirit to quicken you with instinctive affection toward a perfect-fit ministry ordained by God for you.

Can you really pull this off? Of course not. But God can. So ask Him to work through you for His glory.

He is your potter. Ask Him to shape your clay (Isaiah 64:8).

Consider what you want to do and press on. Don't be passive. Seize the Power of Mission. As long as you have breath, it's not too late.

For personal reflection and discussion:

1. In the past, in what way have you felt obligated to fulfill the dreams of others?
2. Do you feel frustrated by being in the wrong career or discouraged that you're on an ill-fitting path? What are you going to do about it?
3. What is the dream buried in your heart?

Chapter Six

OVERCOMING MISSION FATIGUE: Overturn Adversity. Extract Pearls.

At times, your financial path may feel twisted, broken, or nonexistent, even when you're following God's path. What is that about? Maybe there's a glorious reason we cannot see or know. A season of adversity forces us to stretch, as if the invisible hand of God is prodding and pushing us through a doorway into a future we'd never discover on our own. We cry, "How can something so right be going so wrong?" And yet, consider how oysters respond to irritants by producing pearls. Mercifully, the worst circumstances often produce the best blessings, when from our adversity, we too extract pearls. If you're in the midst of a financial or professional jam, take comfort in knowing it's not necessarily evidence of your spiritual condition but of the human condition. Rocky Road isn't just an ice cream flavor—it's the road we're all traveling, this side of Heaven, even when we're walking on the right path.

When going through a trial, how can we cast off the debilitating interference of self-doubt? How can we regain the confidence to get through it? One protective tool, often overlooked, is self-talk. In challenging situations, we sometimes worsen our suffering by our running internal commentary. Let's be sure to tell ourselves the truth. Observe your self-talk, and never allow yourself to be mired in misbelief.

Three Myths About Adversity

When adversity confronts, why are we afraid to confront it right back? Let's target three common falsehoods that needlessly shame us into immobility in troubled times.

I was sinful.

Well, of course you were! As are every one of us. If the only reason for adversity were sin, none of us would survive. Jesus, our Savior, has covered our sins. God sees you as His beloved son or daughter. Sometimes, a perfect parent allows their child to experience difficulty, not as punishment, but for their good. In every circumstance, we're wise to check our sinfulness at the door in repentance and prayer. But once we are forgiven (which happens instantly after we repent), any further voice of condemnation is only a false and misleading distraction sent by the enemy for the purpose of hindering our efforts.

To think clearly, you must turn off every accusing voice.

I was stupid.

There is a big difference between effort and outcome. Effort is what we control. Outcome is beyond our control.

Adversity does not mirror capability. It offers no indication of your future. The present is merely today's snapshot of your project-in-process. Like taking a photo on a bad hair day. You are not stupid. There's more you can and will do. You know more than you did yesterday, and you'll know even more tomorrow.

One of my clients longed to purchase a vacation home as a family fun haven for their grandchildren to gather and create lasting family memories. They saved, prayed, paused, and sought exhaustive counsel. They did all the right things before buying that house. The consensus was that it was a wise decision—and it was.

No one could have predicted their business revenues would plummet fifty percent the following year—and stay down for a decade. This unheard-of scenario forced them into a season of adversity. Still, it was not based on stupidity, only on the human condition. God got them through it, taught them many empowering lessons, and gave them the memory-making home they desired.

I was slothful.

Truly slothful people do not know they are slothful. If you're like most hardworking, mission-driven clients I've served, it's unlikely you were slothful. Taking time off to get a good night's rest, attend a child's sporting event, or enjoy a day of Sabbath rest is not evidence of sloth but of stewardship.

If My Mission is Right, Why Are Things So Wrong?

As you pursue your dream, the enemy of your soul is in unholy pursuit of you. Satan comes to distract, delay, and disrupt you from your God-given dream. Until now, you may have lived gently as a dove. Now, you'll want to live intentionally... shrewd and wildly strategic. Patient, steadfast, and full of faith.

My Adversity. My Pearl.

I'm wired to be an entrepreneur.

I owned my first retail travel agency in my mid-twenties. Wholesaling tours for private groups was my specialty. A decade later, I decided to open a strictly wholesale corporate travel business. This mission made perfect sense. I was highly qualified, experienced, and knew exactly what I was doing. Never was someone as ideally suited to their mission. Or so I thought.

After making a stellar presentation to AT&T, I quickly secured a letter of intent, which, at least in my mind, meant securing unstoppable future success. But I'd been accustomed to quick retail travel transactions—not bureaucratic delays. I hadn't factored in the lengthy time between a corporate *yes* and a corporate *check.* I waited many months for that check. By the end of the year, my little start-up company was so drenched in red ink that I risked losing my home.

Needing a fast cash infusion, I hastily created a seasonal side business: tax preparation. I hung a sign in my street-front office window and placed handmade flyers on cars. It was only temporary, I promised myself—one tax season only.

I felt no joy or excitement about preparing tax returns. In truth, I detested the idea. My reluctant mission was only to earn enough quick cash to keep my *real* business alive. But the hole had been dug too deep, and I soon had to wave the white flag of surrender. I tearfully begged a friend of mine to buy my wholesale business, whose value at that point was nothing more than a hope and a promise. Kindly, she paid me a token two thousand dollars. It was as much an act of charity to sustain, feed, and house me for one more month.

Though doubtful she could steer the business from life support to survival, she spared me the heartbreak of shutting it down. Oh, the irony. Two weeks after that sale, my long-awaited AT&T contract—and very large check—arrived. The speed of her investment payoff was unbelievable. $288,000 in today's dollars was mailed directly to her as the rightful new owner of the company.

God knew precisely when that check would come. It was painfully obvious He did not intend that profit for me. With my dream officially slammed shut, all I had left was this dreaded new tax business. *But Lord, it was supposed to be temporary!*

I didn't feel appointed or anointed for tax work, nor did I sense God providing me with direction, provision, or escape. Hemmed in by a business I detested, I prayed day and night for the Lord to reroute me back to my chosen occupation—which was definitely not income tax. With no apparent rescue from above and no visible alternatives, my only choice was to brace my will and prepare the next tax return.

That first tax season was miserable. In the pre-software age, tax returns were prepared by hand. You actually had to know complicated tax law and be 100% legal and meticulous. There was no software to correct me if I forgot a form, missed a line, or miscalculated.

Worst of all, there was no system to confirm my results were accurate. Though I'd been educated in tax preparation and mentored by several family members in the tax business, I was in this business alone and terrified of making a mistake.

I was also very frustrated—at myself, at the situation I found myself in, and at my clients who had no understanding of what was required. I found myself wincing as I sifted through disorganized shoeboxes of papers. Behind my tired smile, I was joyless. My office window faced beautiful palm trees and a lush Florida landscape, but spiritually and professionally, I was living in the desert.

Tax season number two wasn't nearly as bad. My clients were lovely. Some of those eye-straining, 15-hour days became…well, quite pleasant.

Tax season number three was positively transformative. Deep bonds of mutual trust and caring had formed between my clients and me. Referrals were flowing in like crazy, and revenues were high. I deepened my understanding of tax law's complexities and inconsistencies and was genuinely stimulated and fulfilled in my work.

Then, just as I was beginning to embrace my new mission, my dear clients unsettled me by asking for financial advice. Several tried to hand me six-figure checks they'd received from retirement plans, trusting me to advise them what to do with their entire life savings.

I found this so alarming that my hand recoiled. I had no idea what they should do. "I'm a tax preparer, not a financial planner," I repeatedly protested. Investments were way beyond the scope of my qualifications.

I'd grown to love these clients, and I feared for their vulnerability and sweet naivete. I couldn't bear the thought of them turning to the wrong person for investment advice.

One unforgettable day, after the third client request in a single week, a holy lightning bolt struck the center of my being. *I need to protect these clients! Why am I not a financial planner?*

In a life-transforming moment of mission revelation, I awakened to an excitement I hadn't known possible. An electric current raced through my being, connecting the dots of my past and igniting the dots of my purpose. God's amazing plan was about to unfold.

I returned to school at night. Four years later, I proudly added "CFP" (Certified Financial Planner™) to my business card. By then, I'd built a full book of loyal tax clients in two branch locations, which gave me a tremendous financial advantage: they knew me, trusted me, and couldn't wait to become my investment clients.

God's plan was fantastic. The icing on my spiritual cake! Unlike my previous venture, He spared me from opening a financial planning practice without an immediate revenue stream. Once He'd placed me where He wanted me, He didn't allow me to fail.

For those surrendered to the Lord, God wastes nothing. He used all the sorrow and failure that had forced me to open a tax business to lead me through a doorway into the career He'd ordained from the beginning—a redemptive financial planning career that healed my past—a career I would not have discovered any other way.

I'd been on a good path—a reasonable and appropriate path—but it was not *His* path.

The Lord had to uproot me in order to replant me.

The Lord had to detour me in order to bless me.

That tight hemming in of those early tax seasons was not God's abandonment after all, but His great gift, an exquisite protection to keep me from pursuing any other mission but His.

Three years later, I no longer needed to maintain two businesses. I sold my tax practice for top dollar—but kept my clients. Only God.

I smile as I recall how relentlessly I'd prayed to be rescued from those early wretched tax seasons. But because God loved me, He ignored my plea.

This would not be my last encounter with business or financial adversity, but this was the defining experience that taught me to look beyond the visible and ready myself to extract my pearls. To watch prayerfully and patiently for God's plan to unfold and be ready to jump into blessing.

The details of your missional adversity will be different from mine. But if you call Jesus Lord, His love for you is exactly the same. Try not to be afraid, despite what feels at the time like unanswered prayer. Trust that your days are ordained and your work is appointed.

You won't always know where you're headed—or why. Like me, you'll inevitably encounter setbacks, detours, and impossible obstacles. There may be a failure. Or two. Or three. Don't worry; God will choreograph these to position you perfectly for His holy plan if you ask, trust, and let Him lead you.

All you need to do is stay alert, focus on Him, *and do the next thing,* which means accepting whatever next opportunity He places before you, even if it doesn't seem ideal at the time. We cannot know in advance the complexity of His plan. But this we do know: *"And we know [with great confidence] that God [who is deeply concerned about us] causes all things to work together [as a plan] for good for those who love God, to those who are called according to his plan* and *purpose,"* (Romans 8:28, AMP).

Oh, is it too late for you? At the time of this story, I was not a cute twenty-something just starting out. I was in my mid-thirties, in a crumbling marriage, and without a financial safety net.

In that pivotal season, I didn't have the luxury of deciding what I wanted to do next. I had no options, no choices, no money, and no time. My only safety net was the Lord God. And in the end, He was the only safety net I needed.

When you suffer a season of adversity, when you're struggling in financial or professional darkness, and you don't know what to do…

Do the next thing He places before you.

Though you barely see what is before you and cannot see past the endless twists on the road ahead, turn your gaze heavenward. Be on the lookout to extract your pearl. Take each next step, following His lead, trusting His plan.

You can safely pour out your efforts, trusting Him, the Holy One, your Shepherd, to do what's best for you, whether to slow, stop, divert, or lead you into His highest mission for your life.

Never hesitate to do the next thing He puts before you.

One day, you too may discover it was the next *ordained* thing.

For personal reflection and discussion:

1. In what way has mission fatigue saturated your outlook and dimmed your confidence?
2. How have you been unfairly diverted from a plan you believed was best? Hemmed in by a circumstance that feels insurmountable?
3. What is the next thing God has placed before you to do? Into what waters will you dive to extract your pearl?

Chapter Seven

THE PRINCIPLE OF PERMISSION: Let Your Yes Be Yes

You've dreamed about your passion project…maybe for a very long time.

You've embraced your mission.

Fertilized it with prayer.

Sharpened it with planning.

Safeguarded it with counsel.

You've imagined and creatively replayed its joyous outcome again and again.

After all the endless prayer, planning, and counsel, your next step will determine whether your dream lives—or dies.

Are you ready? Yes, you are.

Time to stop *talking* about your dream—and start *doing* something to make it come true. Give yourself permission to press forward. Begin to *do* instead of *dream*.

All dreams begin with a yes. If we don't let that first, tenuous yes become a steadfast *yes, an unyielding yes* that no scoffer can twist into a *no*, we'll become perpetual dreamers—not actionable doers. God doesn't want you to be a double-minded dreamer. He wants you to commit.

Until you give yourself wholehearted, single-minded permission to commit to your dream, then unfortunately, however noble, needed, or necessary it is, your mission will stall. *"Like clouds and wind without rain is one who boasts of gifts never given,"* (Proverbs 25:14). No more tip-toeing around your challenge. You may never feel ready. But at some point, you must permit yourself to bravely plunge into your purpose.

Whether your mission is to raise a family, an industry, or a flag on a distant planet, the Power of Permission will protect you and project you forward by giving you the resolve to persevere.

Permission is really about commitment, a trait very pleasing to God. *"Commit to the LORD whatever you do, and he will establish your plans,"* (Proverbs 16:3).

To commit will require much from you. It will mean no running away when your challenge seems unmanageable. You'll be forced to draw on reserves of courage, humility, discipline, stewardship, and faith. But these traits are pleasing to God and will draw His blessing over your enterprise.

Until you give yourself wholehearted permission to pursue your dream, you'll question your mission every time you suffer a setback. You'll inaccurately perceive each and every challenge as some sort of signal that you shouldn't be trying at all. Your fruitless speculation about whether to stay or quit will blind you to the potential benefits of powering through these trials. A lack of courageous commitment wastes enticing opportunities to develop muscles of confidence, creativity, and innovation.

Have you ever wondered how wealth-confident people manage to overcome Herculean challenges and achieve big dreams? It's partly because they're not double-minded or dubious when they face their challenges. Their commitment never wavers. Permission is powerful.

Guy took night classes for six months to prepare for his State Insurance license exam. Of the thirty-five in his class, twenty-five failed. Few took the exam again. But Guy did, and this time, he passed. He didn't allow one failure to alter his commitment. By giving yourself wholehearted, single-minded permission to succeed, you can insulate your dreams from inertia, procrastination, and wobbly discouragement. Your unshakable commitment to shake off interference will guard your enterprise against doublemindedness—from tender start to triumphant finish.

Permission is the power of *yes.* A wholehearted, undivided "*yes*" erects invisible boundaries between us and all the distractors, naysayers, time-wasters, and life squanderers encircling us. It signifies an official okay from you to you.

The greater the mission, the greater your challenges will be, but no need to worry because permission is a reliable sustainability tool. When your mission is ambushed by a seemingly unfixable circumstance or set ablaze by a rocket of unexpected rejection, the Power of Permission will scoop your dream into an armored tank of *mission protection* and allow you to plow through the obstacles on your path. You'll experience the exhilaration of perseverance as never before.

The stop-go approach of your double-minded past may have kept you thus far from gaining ground. Your dream now teeters on the edge of something big. Is it a giant breakthrough? Or a cliff? That may well depend on your commitment.

If you can't commit right now, it may be circumstantial, and that's all right. It's possible that at this moment, commitment would do more harm than good. You may be dealing with nobler priorities, such as child-rearing, caregiving, or adapting to a gentle reentry in a new season of life. Commitment is not about rushing the process. It's about trusting the process.

Commitment is not about rushing the process. It's about trusting the process.

Some seasons of life present hard stops for even the noblest of dreams. If, for some reason, at this time, you cannot be *all in,* maybe it's wise to *get out.* Don't waste your days forever in fantasy. For the sake of your future, pack up this dream, along with the paraphernalia associated with it, and move it all into safe, temporary storage to make space in your imagination for another. There are countless cases of dreams that had to be put off for decades until the timing was right. But if this is the mission you're sure you want, and you want it now, then you must commit—fearlessly, faithfully, ferociously.

Why Do We Avoid Commitment?

As soon as we come face-to-face with the notion of committing to our dream, fear rises to the top of our consciousness. We give ourselves many reasons to avoid commitment. Some of those reasons might even be true.

We fear being hasty.

I don't want to be rash, risky, or reckless.

Naturally, those actions would be sinful and foolish. But commitment doesn't mean rushing the godly process of preparation and decision-making.

It only means…

- No more stalling.

- No more obsessive planning.
- No more lingering in daydreams.
- No more fear disguised as perfectionism.

We fear missing God's plan.

Was my dream inspired by God—or by my own imagination?

God doesn't send us a letter. He sends us an opportunity.

- If you're following the Lord, reading His word, and convinced of your life's value in Him (Power of Identity),
- If you've grasped that He has ordained purposes for each of us to perform (Power of Mission),
- If you've prayed and sought counsel (Power of Prayer),

Then it's time to strap on your seatbelt and drive.

We fear being trapped.

How do I know I'll still want this mission ten years from now?

You don't. A *lifetime* is a *long* time. Expect God to inspire you with a new dream one day, a dream you're not yet ready for now.

When He inspires you one day with a new mission, He'll maximize everything you learned from this one—whose purpose may only have been to equip you for the next one. You probably need this mission you're pursuing now as a training ground for the greater one to follow.

Embrace today's mission as an essential steppingstone to a brighter future. *"But the path of the righteous is like the light of dawn That shines brighter and brighter until the full day,"* (Proverbs 4:18, NASB).

We fear taking action.

I need to think about it some more.

It's less stressful to imagine a dream than commit to it. We'd rather talk than act. But consider:

- *"Work brings profit; talk brings poverty!"* (Proverbs 14:23, TLB).
- At some point, we must not talk. We must do.
- Commit to doing something, or you'll do nothing.
- Talking does not grow profit. Actual work is required for that.

We fear failure.

What might the failure of this project do to my reputation? To my future?

Failure has many causes—and many purposes.

Your present dream may fail—*and* also be an essential part of God's fantastic, ordained path to place you exactly where He wants you to be.

If we're called according to His purposes, God promises we can trust Him to work our circumstances together for our good (Romans 8:28).

There are many ways God uses a bad outcome to lift you to a higher advantage:

- To equip you for something even better.

- To steer you in a divine direction.
- To teach you something essential you'll need for even greater success.
- To cause you to meet the right person.
- To encounter a divine opportunity that could come to you no other way.
- To be the best thing that ever happened to you.

When a Disappointment Leads to a Greater Yes

Many years ago, a travel agency signed an exclusive contract to manage the convention travel for a national organization, and they hired me to run it. It was a massive enterprise involving chartering commercial aircraft for pre-and-post-convention side trips and acquiring ten thousand hotel rooms. The project was daunting, the hours insane, but the salary was fabulous, and my contract included a corporate apartment, a company car, and a promised bonus of over one year's salary at convention's end.

By God's grace, the convention was a profitable success. After the closing ceremonies, I slept for two days straight.

And then my employer fled the country with all the convention's profits.

Looking back, I'd begun to notice some disturbing irregularities, such as on two occasions when nondescript-looking men in dark suits walked in the agency's front door, and the owner slipped out the back. Still, I was stunned. Not only had I been swindled out of an entire year's income, but the owner's actions cost me my job, my corporate apartment, and my company car.

It was a devastating crime, to be sure. Every element of my life was decimated, and I had to depend on God for immediate employment, housing, and transportation. Not only did He orchestrate movie-script-worthy miracles, but He also used that financial crime to place me on the dream path He wanted for me.

I was soon given a chance to open a travel agency of my own.

And, through that ordeal, I met the man I would eventually marry. He had been swindled by them too.

What my employer meant for evil, God used for good.

This experience taught me to work hard and without the fear of failure.

God is the One—the only one—who has the authority to set our finish line.

"Whatever you do, do your work heartily, as for the Lord and not for people, knowing that it is *from the Lord* that *you will receive the reward of the inheritance.* It is *the Lord Christ* whom *you serve,"* (Colossians 3:23-24, NASB).

We Fear Success.

What if the only thing you fear more than failure is…success?

If your dream comes true, what will you be forced to confront? Sin? Sorrow? Rejection? We fear success for many good reasons.

- **Financial:** Won't God be angry if I succeed? Aren't Christians supposed to be poor?
- **Familial:** Won't my family and friends be angry, jealous, hurt, or resentful if I succeed? Won't they reject me?
- **Falsehoods:** Won't I be an imposter? What if I'm not smart enough, talented enough, or worthy enough for success?

These fears are intricately intertwined, so let's address them as one.

Those who fall in love with money are indeed in sin—whether they have any money or they don't. Sin is not born from earning or managing money but from the *love* of money. Money is only a tool—God's tool. Honorable earnings are, in fact, encouraged by God to care for our families and to serve His purposes. Success comes from God, not from us. It is God who gives us the ability to produce wealth (Deuteronomy 8:18).

God owns all the money in the world, and He flows some of it through our hands to provide for our needs. Sometimes, He provides extra funds to allow us to partner with Him to meet the needs of His other beloveds around us.

Your venture might be profitable in non-financial ways:

- By providing the satisfaction of helping others.
- By the fulfillment that comes with exercising a talent.
- By knowing you've made a difference in an arena where you've been called.

Your venture might be profitable financially. If so, this is a gift from the Lord, ordained by Him, for His purposes. You are not an imposter; you are a receiver of His unmerited favor. Wealth is not owned by us, nor is it even about us. We are foot soldiers in God's army, working for Him and for His glory.

With this mindset, financial success won't cause you to sin—but rather to listen hard for His instructions. He may allow some profits to remain with you as a gift to reward your hard work and to let you enjoy the dignity of not being dependent on another. You'll feel thankful that you've grown financially in Christ.

This will increase your sensitivity to loved ones and strangers who have not yet attained this freedom.

- You'll be ready to aid them, especially God's beloved widows, orphans, or the elderly in your family.
- You'll be the hands and feet of Jesus, meeting financial needs around you.
- You'll "hover and cover" over others in your life circle who have less.
- You'll quietly absorb extra costs associated with worthy occasions and significant initiatives.

What a joy to partner with God to meet the needs of His beloved. What a privilege to honor God as a faithful steward of the talents and opportunities He's given you.

Five Pillars of Permission

The Power of Permission will help you build mighty support beams to undergird the foundation of your dream. Permission strengthens your resolve by releasing:

- **Courage:** As you raise your hand for the mission and stand tall, ready to act.
- **Commitment:** As you lock your dream securely in place—in launch mode.
- **Stewardship:** As you carefully and responsibly manage the worthy goal entrusted to your care.
- **Discipline:** As you resist the pull and temptation to procrastinate.
- **Humility:** As you relinquish the arrogance of believing you have all the time in the world to pursue your mission.

"Commit your way to the L*ORD; trust in him and he will do this: He will make your righteous reward shine like the dawn, your vindication like the noonday sun,"* (Psalm 37:5-6). *"Do not despise these small beginnings, for the* L*ORD rejoices to see the work begin…"* (Zechariah 4:10, NLT).

For personal reflection and discussion:

1. After working through the powers of identity and mission, are you ready to now give yourself wholehearted permission to pursue your dream?
2. What fears have you identified that you need to confront? How would you confront them?
3. What is the next small step you might take?

Chapter Eight

NEXT LEVEL PERMISSIONS:
Strength for Your Breakthrough

You're striding toward your dream. Good for you! Suddenly, you're stopped by a tall granite structure with a forbidding sign that reads, "The Great Wall of Permission." Wait. Didn't we scale this wall in the last chapter when we shook off our double-mindedness and committed to our dream?

We examine the off-putting structure more closely. We peer at the words etched into stone. Scratched across it are our defenses: pride, dread, embarrassment, humiliation, fear of rejection, loss of control, impatience, shame, and entrenchment.

Oh, no. Not those. There is only one reason we'd consider confronting such dreaded emotions: Our dreams are on the other side of this wall. We have no choice. To attain our best, we have to overcome our worst.

This is it—our chance to confront our last residue of resistance—and topple it with truth. The way we'll break through our wall and unleash success is by permitting ourselves to do seven things not on anyone's dream list:

- Look foolish
- Change
- Change course
- Pick ourselves up after a fall
- Be imperfect
- Press a reset button
- Do what we cannot do

Please don't say, "I can't." If you do, it will spread like a virus into every aspect of your life. It will compromise your confidence. You'll soon hear yourself saying, *I can't cope, handle, pursue, analyze, grow, change, or persevere.* None of these statements are biblical. They are evil. We have an adversary working against us, seeking to steal, kill, and destroy God's elect. Scripture tells us to put on the whole armor of God (Ephesians 6:10-18).

Do not let him win. Rise to the next level. Break through this final remnant of your wall.

Next Level Permissions

Permission to Look Foolish

None of us wants to perform poorly. We all want the world to see us at our best. The only way we can become accomplished is through faithful practice. Don't set aside your tasks, waiting for that day when you excel. Set aside your pride instead. It's not easy—yet—but it will become easier and may eventually become effortless.

As we begin a new initiative, though giving our all, we must permit ourselves to not be very good at first and maybe even look a little foolish. Kids have this concept down cold. They're constantly learning new things they're not very good at, from riding a bicycle without training wheels to studying mathematics. Unlike us, they're willing to look foolish as they try.

I recall my fear of looking foolish as I stepped up to the podium for the first time after a twelve-year hiatus. As my host introduced me, I frantically prayed for a miraculous transformation from my prior day's lackluster rehearsal, but I experienced no such blessing. Throughout my talk, my gaze remained stubbornly glued to my notes instead of on my audience. Instead of connecting with them, I was reading my text, yet I still managed to leave out the best parts. I did so poorly that I feared I'd wrecked God's wonderful message.

Afterward, I sought to make a hasty escape to my car, but a woman rushed at me in tears. She said my talk came straight from Heaven and aimed directly at her. Through sobs, she poured out details of her financial dilemma, and we hugged, cried, and prayed together.

Despite my stumbling delivery and embarrassing performance, the Lord allowed my audience to hear what they needed. To my amazement, I even received referrals from this most awful speaking event ever.

You don't have enough time to fully refine your skills before you act on your dream. You must start where you are. If you do your very best, practice like crazy, and are willing to look a little foolish at first, God will meet you where you are. He'll help those you're trying to bless to receive what they need from imperfect you.

Permission to Change

Don was a pastor whose biblical foundation was thick—and whose skin was thin. It took little for him to erupt into angry outbursts that damaged his relationships. He managed to control himself in the pulpit, but not so much at home. His family, whom he hoped would be his most ardent supporters, kept their polite distance because they were frequently nursing wounds from Don's latest outburst. "There has to be a better way to live in harmony with imperfect loved ones," Don thought.

Sinking into depression, Don finally began to wonder if he was the one who needed to change. Maybe if he accepted them, he might inspire them. Finally, he surrendered his temperament to the Lord, praying his family would begin to trust him as a changed husband and father. They did. His relationships are thriving. His dream for his family is finally coming true.

Permission to Change Course

Jackie's housing arrangement was spiritually harmful and potentially hazardous to her child. She knew God wanted her to extricate herself from her ungodly entanglement, but to do so would require reserves of cash and courage she did not have. There were so many issues to resolve, it seemed risky and foolish to even try. But once she gave herself permission to make the break, God started opening new doors—including the door to her very own apartment.

David loved to cook. After culinary school, he was thrilled for his opportunity to open a small restaurant. His dream soon turned into a nightmare. The business demands of restaurant ownership left little time for the only thing he loved to do: prepare and serve exquisite food. Though restaurant ownership had seemed a considerable rung up the financial ladder, it robbed him of his purpose. After months of angst and prayer, he permitted himself to change course. He tested the waters as a private, in-home chef, catering high-end gourmet dinners for private client parties—and fell in love with his profession again. His purpose roared—and profits soared.

Permission to Pick Yourself Up

You know the feeling. You've been sucker-punched, and you cannot breathe.

The business that couldn't fail—did.

The loved one who would never disappoint—did.

The ministry that was going to rescue—did not.

Emotionally, you're on the floor and want to stay there, thank you. You're done trying, believing, expecting anything good from anyone around you.

But stand up, please. Look to the Heavens. Take the aerial view.

Man's rejection was never intended to be your *stalemate.*

Man's rejection is God's *protection.*

"Therefore put on the full armor of God, so that when the day of evil comes, you may be able to stand your ground, and after you have done everything, to stand," (Ephesians 6:13).

"…for though the righteous fall seven times, they rise again, but the wicked stumble when calamity strikes," (Proverbs 24:16).

You're not wicked. You're righteous.

Give yourself permission to pick yourself up.

Permission to Be Imperfect

If only we could be a little more perfect, everything would work out just fine. That's what we tell ourselves. But it shall never be, and for good reason: God wants us to glorify Him—not ourselves.

Luisa owned a profitable housekeeping business—a perfect fit for one with a passion for cleanliness. She was gifted in solving any cleaning issue or sanitizing any surface. Dirt feared her. But Luisa's perfectionism was turning away her clients because she insisted on time-consuming, perfectionistic detail that cost too much. She would lovingly spend twelve hours or more cleaning a medium-sized home she'd just cleaned the week before. Though her clients respected her commitment to out-clean and outshine all competitors, they were unwilling to pay for more hours than they could afford.

Very few people are willing to pay for perfection. We do our best, as is appropriate for the situation, and rest in that. This is what we teach our children when they play sports, and we need to accept it in our grown-up lives.

Give yourself permission to be imperfect, and you'll break through the wall that keeps you from moving forward.

Permission to Press the Reset Button

"I've gone too far. I can't turn around now," said Bud, walking stoically into a future he dreaded—because he felt too entrenched in his lifestyle to make a wholesale change to his faith walk. Bud finally saved his life by giving himself permission to press the reset button and start anew.

Perhaps the trajectory of your life is off track. You keep searching, adding, trying, and doing, but nothing works. You're reading every book, searching for answers, but no answer is large enough to cover the hole within.

Don't abandon your ordained place on this earth, for no one else can replace you. You are fearfully and wonderfully made. There is one and only *you*.

It is never too late. Even a reset button you press later in life can rescue you from a path of sorrow. I don't know your past, but I do know you can finish well. Your history is not your destiny—unless you invite it to be.

Your history is not your destiny— unless you invite it to be.

Do you long to live a good life? An *I-know-why-I-am-here* life?

Sometimes, you have to press the spiritual reset button and start over. You cannot add to what God has for you—but you can protect what God has for you. Pressing the spiritual reset button is not a self-improvement directive. But once you press it, your outside circumstances will begin to change immediately. *"Brothers and sisters, I do not consider myself yet to have taken hold of it. But one thing I do: Forgetting what is behind and straining toward what is ahead,"* (Philippians 3:13).

Why live the rest of your life on the default track of the flawed human race? Wouldn't you like to return to the holy track for which you were born? Pressing the reset button may mean the difference between life and death.

You can experience a spiritual reset in moments and make an immediate change in the entire trajectory of your life. I did that some years ago. Pressing the spiritual reset button was the most profound decision I ever made, impacting not only my eternal destiny but also the fullness of all my years on this earth.

I've had good and bad days under the remarkable protection of an amazing Father, Son, and Holy Spirit. His gifts, grace, and outright miracles are more than I would dare to ask or even dream (Ephesians 3:20).

You may believe you're so entrenched within an alternate spiritual path or culture that you can't possibly leap over that high wall of entrenchment to meet the Lord, but it's not true. No leaping is required. He'll meet you where you are and walk you right through it.

It's as simple as a prayer. *"Lord, I've tried so hard, but nothing is working. I've sinned against You a thousand times. Please forgive my sins. I was trying to make my way and survive my path, but this path is not the path to life—I see that now—and I don't want to travel on it anymore. Would You forgive and erase my past and help me start over? If I turn away from the culture I've been chained to, would You adopt me into Your family of faith? I can no longer be the lord of my own life. But to whom will I turn? I need You. Jesus, please save me."*

The spiritual reset button is available to all of us. An entirely new life can overlay your former life at any age and under any circumstance. This isn't hopeful thinking. This is glorious truth.

The most life-affirming thing you can do is press the reset button.

Permission to Do What You Cannot Do

January 2009. Captain Chesley B. Sullenberger took off from LaGuardia Airport on USAir #1549. The aircraft under his command was losing altitude and heading straight down. This emergency meant certain death for him and all those under his command, including his flight crew and hundreds of passengers. All would likely die in the next few moments, but Captain "Sully" willed himself to remain calm. Undistracted by runaway emotion, he remained critically alert, and even in the moment of indescribable panic, he was ready to contemplate and seize wildly creative opportunities.

I can imagine how his mind raced swiftly and coolly from option number one through option number five during the three-minute life-and-death ordeal.

"Okay, I have to land. Nearest airport. No, can't make it. Short landing strip. Can't make it. Okay, I'll land on the water. I won't surrender. I'll lift the nose and put it down. I'll do what I have to do. We'll make it work."

Sully never surrendered to the inevitable. Clear-headed and focused, he strategized and calculated; he fought to the very last second, always intentional about winning over a seemingly impossible situation. One hundred fifty-five people are extremely grateful he did.

Most of us are easily derailed by lesser emergencies. Most of us have tomorrow. Sully had only seconds.

With God's help, Sully accomplished something that had never been done before. With God's help, you and I can accomplish something we've never done before. Permit yourself to do what you cannot do without God's help.

After Sully's three-minute flight ordeal was over and all the passengers were safely on terra firma, there was great exhilaration among passengers, crew, and the public at large. When we somehow push through an event we dreaded and discover it didn't have the power to destroy us, we grow more confident. We strengthen our faith and courage.

Promise yourself you'll never surrender to your challenges. Permit yourself to follow through with ordained initiatives you know you cannot complete without God's mighty intervention. In this way, your dream will glorify God.

For personal reflection and discussion:

1. What limiting belief has held you back from pursuing your dream? What is etched on your wall?
2. What must you give yourself permission to do to break through the last remnant of your wall?
3. What is your specific prayer as you face this fear with courage?

Chapter Nine

THE PRINCIPLE OF EXCELLENCE:
Fuel Your Dreams

Excellence turns casual observers into raving fans. What a powerful way to launch your enterprise, ministry, project, or dream.

Excellence is a magnet that woos clients, colleagues, customers, donors, voters, investors, and new friends. It's an attractant that permeates the atmosphere of resistant circumstances and difficult people around you. It causes people to lower their guard—and raise their trust.

Excellence validates your credibility more than any chart, graph, or statistic ever will. It makes people feel safe with you. After you earn their trust, they lay down their defenses and listen to what you have to say.

Whether you're offering the financial profit of investing in your enterprise or you're offering the spiritual profit of salvation, if people trust you, they will hear what you say and be interested in what you recommend. They're more likely to accept your product, plea, or plan.

Excellence makes you stand out—and inspires people to look up. They can't help but wonder what—or, in our case, Who—is motivating you.

Excellence makes your relationships satisfying and profitable. It inspires clients, customers, and colleagues to refer you, propelling your enterprise forward. *"The hand of the diligent will rule…"* (Proverbs 12:24a, NASB).

Excellence Makes Us Stand Out

The first quality I noticed about Guy was the excellence with which he executed everything asked of him. Others saw it too. From his attentive note-taking in meetings to the accuracy of his actions to the fullness of his follow-through, his deeply embedded work ethic captured everybody's attention—on both sides of the conference table.

Even more impressive was that his effort, unlike mine, didn't stem from professional obligation. For him, this was a voluntary civic project. He wasn't there for profit, praise, or glory. Yet still, he gave his all. He worked as if he were working for God and not for men. He showed all of us who he really was.

As a travel wholesaler managing convention travel for their civic organization's upcoming national convention, I spent my days chartering commercial aircraft, creating tours, and arranging ten thousand hotel rooms for conventioneers. My stress was high, and support was minimal. I had no time for mediocrity.

He was one of a five-member leadership team serving as my client liaison. Though at least a dozen of us usually attended meetings, few were noteworthy. Their efforts were lackluster. By contrast, Guy stood out.

- His follow-through was excellent and handled impeccably.
- He disciplined his mood, manners, and management of countless details.
- He was faithful in fulfilling every promise—on time.

- He was even-tempered in complex crises, of which this project had plenty.
- He outworked his peers on the leadership team month after month.
- He spoke respectfully to everyone and was always a gentleman.

Through the Power of Excellence, you can stand out from any crowd of peers, volunteers, or competitors. Your excellent efforts will elevate your status from "one of many" to "*the one* to get it done."

Excellence Makes Profit

Guy was one of nineteen thousand franchisees who sold:

- The same product.
- Through the same process.
- Under the same rules and regulations.
- In the same format.
- To the same public.

Still, *his* franchise rose to the top 1% of those nineteen thousand peers. He held that extraordinary peak for over fifty years.

Everybody who met him wanted to work with him and do business with him. It was obvious that if he chose to deliver this level of excellence even while working as an unpaid volunteer, they could trust him in business—no matter what kind of business he happened to be in.

This demonstrates the amazing profit potential of delivering excellence:

- His product didn't matter.
- His brand didn't matter.
- His price didn't matter.

If Guy stood behind it, everybody knew they'd be safe standing behind him.

The godless win trust through treachery. God's people win trust through excellence, which is more sustainable—relationally, professionally, and financially—than any marketing campaign can ever be.

Excellence Makes Discipline Desirable

Discipline is your superpower. It is the innerspring on which excellence rests. Discipline advances your prospects for success in every sphere of your life.

Is your goal to lead a team, a church, a family, a business, a corporation, or a country? How will you do that if you don't first learn to lead and discipline yourself? "Better…one with self-control than one who takes a city," (Proverbs 16:32).

If we don't rule ourselves, others will rule us. We'll march to their drumbeat and dance to their tune. God doesn't want us to be ruled—except by Him.

Discipline is not a way to need God less—but to honor Him more. Paul said, *"For the Spirit God gave us does not make us timid, but gives us power, love, and **self-discipline**,"* (2 Timothy 1:7, emphasis added). We firm up our will to place under control those things He expects us to control; namely, our willful, fearful, impulsive, procrastinating human tendencies.

Discipline is a high-yield way to live. It empowers us to keep our word, build our reputation, and attract trust and respect. Its payoff is huge.

It's a reliable predictor of future success that creates powerful transformation in every part of your life.

How Do We Activate Discipline?

No one is born disciplined. We develop this capability through practice and repetition—if we want to succeed. The wealth-confident use this formula:

1. They remember what they want *most*—and *why* they want it—in that fleeting moment when they're tempted to accept something less.
2. In weak or tempting moments, they pray for God's instant help (Hebrews 4:15).
3. They protect their "yes" by guarding their "no."

We'll never do it perfectly. And that's perfectly okay. But we must try because a lack of self-discipline thwarts our effectiveness and renders us incapable of creating the successful lives we seek. *"Like a city whose walls are broken through is a person who lacks self-control,"* (Proverbs 25:28).

Thankfully, the Lord is aware of our wrestling match with our human nature, and He's ready to help us. *"No temptation has overtaken you that is not common to man. God is faithful, and he will not let you be tempted beyond your ability, but with the temptation he will also provide the way of escape, that you may be able to endure it,"* (1 Corinthians 10:13, ESV).

Excellence Makes People Look Up

A defining characteristic of our Christian walk is to glorify God through excellence in our work ethic, business activities, and godly interactions with others.

By delivering excellence in our effort, honesty, character, and follow-through, we cause people to pause. What is driving our excellence? This invites opportunities to share our faith and minister Jesus to our hurting world. When we're faithful over little, He gives us much (Matthew 25:21).

The Bible tells us, *"...Always be prepared to give an answer to everyone who asks you to give the reason for the hope that you have..."* (1 Peter 3:15).

The Power of Excellence glorifies God. Its effects span into the Heavens. *"In the same way, let your light shine before others, that they may see your good deeds and glorify your Father in heaven,"* (Matthew 5:16).

Excellence Makes Dreams Come True

After Guy's impoverished childhood, he was determined to crash through the barriers blocking his prospects for success. He made the most of any and every opportunity God gave him, and he trusted his Lord to take care of the rest. *"Whatever your hand finds to do, do it with all your might..."* (Ecclesiastes 9:10a).

The Power of Excellence helped him sustain his courage. He knew his success didn't depend on being ***the*** best—he only needed to be ***his*** best, give ***his*** best, and fulfill ***his*** calling with utmost integrity. Guy's payoff for mastering his skill and his will was fascinating. His circle of success continuously widened. Friendships expanded. Prominent influencers invited him to meet their peers, sit on directors' boards, and serve in leadership positions. These engagements grew his relationships, his business, and his profits.

Excellence will do the same for you. Through excellence, you can multiply your results one hundredfold—or more. And it comes with a promise: *"Do you see someone skilled in their work? They will serve before kings…"* (Proverbs 22:29).

Is Excellence Worth the Effort?

The alternative to excellence is mediocrity. (Yawn.) Sure, it's easier, but it's powerless to thrill, excite, or motivate anyone to…

Support you.

Hire you.

Refer you.

Vote for you.

Buy from you.

Work for you.

Partner with you.

Remember you.

Mediocrity is a low-wattage way to live. It lacks the light to illuminate your talent, the heat to melt resistance, or the fire to incinerate obstacles blocking your path. And face it: mediocrity is boring, both to you and everybody you serve.

While mediocrity flatlines your future, excellence breathes life into every aspect of your mission. It floodlights your presence and platform. Its fire ignites opportunity like a match on wood. Excellence makes life exciting, for you and everyone around you.

We're all time-constrained and understandably tempted to offer less of ourselves to jobs or tasks we dislike or activities we deem of lower status.

Yet, as light illuminates darkness, the lesser the task, the more noteworthy the excellent effort. The assignment may be unimpressive—but excellence is always impressive.

God wants us to give our all to everything we set our hand to do. Sure, we can get by with mediocrity—but we won't get ahead. As Christ-followers, whatever we do, we do in the name of the Lord Jesus (Colossians 3:17). It would be better to say no to a task than to give less than our best.

Whether we're on the fast track to our dreams or off-track and praying for His rescue…*"Whatever you do, do your work heartily, as for the Lord and not for people, knowing that* it is *from the Lord* that *you will receive the reward of the inheritance.* It is *the Lord Christ* whom *you serve,"* (Colossians 3:23-24, NASB).

Is the Power of Excellence worth the effort? Hard yes.

For personal reflection and discussion:

1. Name someone you admire whose excellence has caused them to stand out. How have they inspired you? What question would you like to ask them?
2. What is the hardest part about discipline? What strategy will you use to embrace and conquer that hard part?
3. What motivates you toward excellence in your noble pursuit?

Chapter Ten

THE ART OF FINANCIAL ELEGANCE

We're all instinctively drawn to elegance. We long to surround ourselves with it, fill our lives with it, revel in it, and exude it to others.

We gaze wistfully at those blessed with assets such as brains, beauty, talent, wealth, and opportunity, presuming elegance is beyond our reach. But the art of financial elegance requires none of these attributes.

Are you financially elegant? We recognize financial elegance immediately when we see it. But what is it? Merriam-Webster defines elegance as "refined grace or dignified propriety. Dignified gracefulness or restrained beauty of style. Neatness and simplicity."[2]

> Elegance doesn't require talent, only discipline.
>
> Elegance doesn't require brains, only habits.
>
> Elegance doesn't require wealth, only willingness.
>
> Elegance doesn't require opportunity—it creates it.

2 "elegance." Merriam-Webster.com. November 8, 2024. https://www.merriam-webster.com/dictionary/elegance.

> Elegance isn't something to which we aspire. It's something to which we commit.
>
> Elegance doesn't require beauty, for it is its own beauty.
>
> Elegance is God's way of doing business.

In our previous chapter, we explored the Power of Excellence, which supports us like a fine bed on an innerspring of discipline. Elegance is the exquisite bedding artfully arrayed on top. We cannot drape elegance over an unmade bed.

Elegance is a refined and graceful way of interacting with all the resources God provides, whether modest—or much. The coveted attributes of brains, beauty, talent, wealth, and opportunity are meaningless to create elegance, nor can we purchase it for any price. Yet, even if you are not wealthy—*or not yet wealthy*—you can live elegantly.

Edward and Mimi's Unmatched Elegance

Edward and Mimi are the most financially elegant couple I've ever known. When they became my clients, they were ministry workers of modest means. Yet their finances were elegant. Their habits were elegant. Their lifestyle was elegant. Their countenance was elegant. Their commitment to Christ in every financial moment was elegant.

The rhythms of their lifestyle were harmonious and exquisite. Their financial processes were smooth and organized, disciplined and timely. No last-minute rush to do what could have or should have been done before.

Edward and Mimi lived elegantly. Their financial routines were orderly. There was no chaotic spending. They lived within their humble means—what an elegant way to live. They saved. They gave. They prepared. They even planned for their children's college educations.

The ministry that employed them provided housing, which helped keep costs down. But when its leadership changed, their positions were eliminated. They lost their jobs and their housing on the same day. Some might wonder if God had forsaken them. He hadn't.

They secured new jobs but needed a place to live, praying the Lord would help them find a home before the start of school for their two teenage daughters.

In true Ephesians 3:20-style, God merged their limited savings with His unlimited resources and provided a gorgeous three-bedroom, two-bath house in a lovely neighborhood. It would be their first experience owning a home. Such a stunning display of God-math reminds us how God can bless us even when the numbers don't add up.

To furnish it, they had a choice: they could charge the expense—or charge the throne of God in prayer. They decided to pray and wait. Miraculously, a widow moving out of her home wanted to bless someone who would treasure the blessing entrusted them with her entire household of designer furniture. True story.

When their daughters left for college, they made the prayerful decision to turn one bedroom into an overnight guest rental, which generated several thousand dollars monthly to meet expenses. In their eyes, it was an opportunity ordained by God to minister love and Christlike hospitality to people from around the world.

Edward and Mimi saved faithfully, spent purposefully, and gave generously. When their old car needed to be replaced, they gave it to a single mom.

Elegance flows into every part of our lives and draws respect, so it was no surprise when Mimi was offered a significant promotion and substantial raise.

Since they've chosen to work in ministry rather than for wealth, they will never be rich but live wisely and well. They love their jobs and employers. Their home is beautiful. God has truly blessed Edward and Mimi.

To prepare for retirement, they're actively working to pay off their mortgage. How elegant of them. This discipline will reward them with an elegant post-retirement lifestyle. With no mortgage, credit card, or auto debt, their expenses will be low, so their lifestyle can feel high on much less.

In twenty-five years of financial services, I've worked with clients at every wealth level imaginable, but never have I witnessed elegance like this.

From Wealth to Wreckage

Wealth will not provide elegance if we live chaotic, impulsive, inelegant lifestyles. Many wealthy and famous people, including lottery winners, die poor after adopting lifestyles of reckless and inelegant financial interactions—with no rein on spending. No savings. No cushion. No financial margin. They bypass all the wonderful wealth instructions in the Bible. How sad.

If financial elegance is not a part of their wealth story, no degree of fame or fortune will save them.

The Price of Elegance

Some mistakenly believe that elegance costs a great deal of money. They're waiting for an inheritance, jackpot, or successful venture. But financial elegance is unrelated to wealth. It has nothing to do with money.

Elegance is an outward expression of an inner lifestyle.

> *Elegance isn't a consequence—it's a decision.*

It isn't about money but mindset.

It isn't about a sum but a system.

It isn't about a figure but a flawless interaction with whatever amount you have.

Elegance doesn't come after wealth—it invites it.

It doesn't follow—it leads.

Elegance isn't a consequence—it's a decision.

Who Were You Before?

Wealth doesn't create elegance. It reveals it. If you want to be elegant, you can start living elegantly today, right where you are.

Elegance comes from within. Past circumstances may have distorted your financial identity without you even knowing. If so, the concept of financial elegance may not resonate with you.

Were you born on the wrong side of the tracks? You can switch tracks. Today. Elegance is possible for everyone at every financial level, starting right now.

Is your financial identity bruised or damaged? Begin your identity-building process immediately. Reclaim your true self based on God's truth—about you.

Your financial identity is something to preserve, protect, safeguard, and defend. *"The thief comes only to steal and kill and destroy; I have come that they may have life, and have it to the full,"* (John 10:10).

Before life went wrong, who did God create you to be? Who were you before?

You know…

Before you got angry?

Before you got hurt?

Before you were rejected?

Before you were frightened?

Before you were struck down?

Before you had a loss?

Before you were sad?

Before you failed?

If your true self has been beaten down, you may need an identity repair. Or bypass. Or upgrade. You may need to trade in your old identity for a new one. Can you do that?

Yes. You can. And you must.

No one will know *how* you did it—or *that* you did it—but they will immediately begin to respond differently to your new way of doing business with life…God's way. Upgrade to an identity of godly financial elegance, and it will flow through every part of your life, impacting your job, relationships, financial confidence, clarity, and contentment.

Cultivating an elegant lifestyle is easier than you think.

It's not about math—but mindset.

It's not about desire—but a decision to handle your finances smoothly and consistently.

Though the numbers differ for each of us, the path is the same.

How to Invite and Model Financial Elegance

Simplicity and Grace

Simplicity is elegant. Clutter is not. Financial chaos is not an elegant way to live.

The opposite of financial elegance isn't poverty—it's sloppiness—in our financial character, countenance, and transactions.

Cleanliness is elegant. Not the cleanliness of removing dust from our living room, but removing debris from our lifestyle. We thought our financial flaws were safely closeted out of view. We were mistaken. An elegant, wealth-confident life is an inside-out affair. By streamlining our paper, possessions, and processes, we invite elegance.

Integrity and Honor

Integrity and honor express elegance; beyond that, they may invite wealth. Integrity exhibits spiritual richness and character that people perceive as elegance. Promises made and kept inspire respect and awe. When others regard us as honorable and elegant, they entrust us with high levels of responsibility.

Routines and Rhythms

Intention is elegant. Impulse is not.

Orderly financial rhythms are central to financial elegance. *"For God is not a God of disorder but of peace..."* (1 Corinthians 14:33a). Disorder is not an elegant way to live.

Ways We Model Financial Elegance

...In consistency of financial patterns and routines, including saving, spending, giving, and managing debt. Consistency is elegant, inspiring trust and producing momentum.

...In calendared routines for all financial matters, such as bill paying, income tax payments, and monthly assessments of finances. Elegance is knowing the state of our flocks.

...In saving for the unknowns. Regular saving and giving are the hierarchies of an elegant and wealth-confident life. Saving maintains elegance when the unexpected occurs.

...In patterns of thrift, especially over smaller expenditures, to quietly and elegantly open funds for what matters most.

...In planning. Planning is elegant. Unpreparedness is not. Wise men and women plan for the future (Proverbs 21:20).

Harmony and Refinement

Harmony pleases our senses and models refinement and elegance. Disruption and discord are like off-notes in a loud symphony, disturbing us deeply and interrupting focus and momentum.

Elegant decisions sweeten and strengthen our lives. Inner coordination of God's financial truths empowers outer financial harmony, freeing money to flow smoothly and rhythmically.

Refinement emerges in a smooth process, a stately rhythm, and a dignified financial life patterned with consistency, not checkered with careless mistakes. The steps of financial elegance are smooth and sure.

How to Sustain Elegance in Times of Adversity

George and Pamela attained affluence until a dark financial chapter descended. They handled it with elegance.

- They stopped all discretionary spending without grumbling or complaining.
- They postponed replacing their cars.
- They refused to borrow what they needed, trusting God to provide whatever He wanted them to have.

Three practices they chose *not* to forsake were saving, tithing, and Christ-centered giving. Instead of dropping these essential godly rhythms, they dropped the extras...like fine dining and luxury travel. When they needed to get away, a former European vacation became a one-night stay at a local hotel.

They simplified the framework of their lifestyle, choosing to regard this season as a healthy pruning, electing curiosity over complaint.

They maintained fluid financial elegance, even though they were unsure they'd ever be able to return to their former way of life.

At some point, their situation reversed. The Lord brought them through their season of financial adversity, and they made a graceful reentry into affluence. They were surprised they no longer wanted some of their former pleasures. However, they replaced their cars, attended to much-overdue home improvements, and rejoiced in a spectacular home renovation. Generosity, which had been carefully maintained, was joyfully magnified.

Overall, there had been no significant change in their lifestyle, and many of their peers never knew what they'd endured.

Separating Your Past From Your Elegant Future

In the past…

- You may have dismissed elegance as pretension. Now you embrace elegance as a reflection of humility, grace, and intention.
- You may have believed that an elegant financial life is the consequence of a great start. Now you know that even those who start poorly can finish well.
- You may have wondered if creating an elegant life depended on forces outside your control. Now you know that financial elegance comes from within.
- You may have feared elegance might be fleeting in times of adversity. Now you know how to build a sustainable, elegant infrastructure that no storm will wash away.

Financial elegance is a refined grace: a calming, content way to live that uplifts and enriches your life experience at every financial level. Its presence creates a climate that invites and attracts desirable relationships, job opportunities, and wealth.

At its heart, wealth-confidence is really about holy elegance and the courage to manage your big life for the glory of God.

Choose elegance. Choose to live a lifestyle of godly financial elegance. Align yourself with God's truths about who you were made to be and how God made you to live so you can finally get on with the holy business of earning, building, growing, and giving.

An elegant lifestyle will steer you toward the right spouse, career, business, income, friends, and life path. You can rightly position yourself to attract and not repel heavenly opportunities, genuine productivity, and authentic success—financial and otherwise.

The time to begin is today.

For personal reflection and discussion:

1. What aspect of elegance most stands out to you? Intrigues you?
2. Define how cultivating financial elegance will change how you interact with God and money.
3. What is the next step you will take?

Chapter Eleven

THE PRINCIPLE OF STRATEGY: Design Your Master Blueprint

Now that you've secured the foundational powers of identity, mission, permission, and excellence, you're ready to design a highly detailed, well-developed blueprint. Strategy is a powerful component of success. It's an indispensable tool that shows you exactly how to move forward. You may not know precisely how to create it, but you won't be doing it alone. God is with you. *"Commit to the LORD whatever you do, and he will establish your plans,"* (Proverbs 16:3).

What is Strategy?

A strategy is an action plan. It changes the status of your dream from fuzzy fantasy to actionable enterprise.

Strategy doesn't rely on chance, fate, or uncooperative others because it's not a wish list—it's an action list. Your strategy doesn't define what you hope somebody else will do. It outlines what you alone will do to attain your objective.

By quantifying, itemizing, and prioritizing each step ahead, you'll effectively hone and refine your mission. Creating a blueprint helps you envision your enterprise with clarity. By drawing a map, you set into motion all the steps and tasks to drive you to your goal. A crystal-clear strategy puts your foot on the accelerator.

The Four Corners of Successful Strategy

It's best to approach your strategy as if it's a complex jigsaw puzzle—by placing your corners first. Strategize: Your concept. Your steps. Your time. Your anticipated challenges.

Strategize Your Concept: Outthink

Where will you find the outflow of fresh ideas to mold and shape unique concepts for your winning enterprise? Not in the retread of thoughts sitting atop your consciousness. You'll have to mine them from a deeper place—a place most of us don't often visit.

We are woefully under-exercised in deep, solution-based thinking. We're not lazy—we're just distracted, overstimulated, and much too busy.

In our attention deficit, low-concentration culture, our phones and devices have turned us into superficial multitaskers. We've forgotten how to think deeply.

By necessity, we skate the surface of thoughts while juggling the hectic pace of everyday life. Superficial thinking gets us through the day but does not help us create the winning strategies we need. We must go deeper.

The only way to design courageous and innovative new twists, ideas, and variations for our enterprise is to move beyond the banal. We must bypass the trivial, transient, temporal thoughts and images that flit constantly across our devices and minds. Only then will a winning strategy become crystal clear.

Deep thinking is a lost art worth relearning. There's nothing hocus-pocus about it. It's simply focusing our thoughts to explore creative territory we've not stretched our minds to imagine before. Once we do, we'll encounter a wide-open prairie of fresh alternatives and ideas.

When we read biographies of great innovators like Albert Einstein, Thomas Edison, and the Wright brothers, we learn how they hyper-focused on wildly creative possibilities and disciplined their brains to imagine and reimagine every equation to solve their problems. We don't need their brilliance. We need their focus.

To actualize the dreams in our hearts, we must quiet ourselves and learn to think deeply, like they did. There's an undeveloped panorama of possibility for those of us willing to think.

Strategize Your Steps: Out Plan

Your goal may be big, bold, and broad—to start a ministry, a company, or a family—but your strategy needs to be small, narrow, and tight...

- well-defined
- minutely detailed
- actionable—not dreamy
- adaptable to constant tweaking and adjusting

When planning your steps, think small. Design each action to be as bite-sized as possible—a task you can complete in an hour or a day. Tiny steps keep you from becoming pressured or overwhelmed or putting off a fearful task that feels overwhelming. Crossing off completed tasks grows confidence and refuels momentum, energizing us to reach for the next…and next…and next.

Take Guy, for example. Guy steps into every strategy as if it's a military operation. He knows exactly what he will do next. Though he has no guarantee it will work, he guarantees to himself that he'll execute every single action he's meticulously planned.

Remember to invite God into your process. *"In their hearts humans plan their course, but the LORD establishes their steps,"* (Proverbs 16:9).

Strategize Your Time: Outwork

Aim to outwork everybody around you—*not* in hours, but in effectiveness.

When you're working, make every hour count.

The Power of GPS

Keep a written, constantly updated action sheet in front of you. Use it as a dynamic GPS to track…

- where you are
- where you hoped you'd be at this point
- where you need to be at today's close
- your next action, turn, or move
- your goal date for arriving at your destination

Your enterprise is like football, and you are the star player. Football is a game of inches and so is the process of creating a successful business. Your goal is to make plays and run yards. On the best days, you'll score touchdowns. On other days, you'll run ten yards for a first down. But every day—without exception—whether in inches, yards, or across a one-hundred-yard field, you'll work to move forward. Be sure to keep a written record of your "stats," your testimony of what God helped you accomplish. This will glorify Him. Every time you look at it, your confidence will surge.

Set Your Boundaries

It's essential from the outset to establish fair and wise boundaries. The structural details of your life may conspire against you. Don't allow the whims of others to steal your chance to make progress.

Throughout an unproductive week, Dan, in frustration, tracked every interruption he'd endured. This simple exercise proved that his battle was real—not imagined or exaggerated. Until he took charge, he knew next week would be no different.

Dan pinpointed the source of his distress: unceasing and unreasonable requests by others that he always met with a compliant "yes." He needed to find his "no" and a way to express it without angering his employer or alienating his peers. Maybe you need to do the same.

By establishing your boundaries, you'll no longer respond with annoyance when others ask for more than you can give. You'll be able to decline that which you must with sincere warmth and genuine regret instead of frustration or anger because, at last, you'll know you are in charge.

"I would love to…do that…go there…help you out…say yes…"

- "…but I must complete the tasks I've already promised."
- "…but I do not have the bandwidth to take on your worthy project."
- "…but I cannot because God has called me to something else. I do not want to disappoint you—but I cannot disappoint Him."

We cannot expect others to secure our boundaries. This responsibility belongs to us alone. Jesus didn't do everything people asked of Him, but He did the one crucial thing that saved us.

Sometimes, we play the dangerous game of writing more *time checks* than we have hours to cover. We sacrifice sleep, sanity, and sacred rest. Timewise, we become overdrawn—and overwrought. We might get away with this—for a while. Eventually, we collapse into burnout…of our health, joy, and purpose.

Jesus didn't live this way. He rested. He had a short three years to change the world. Yet, He rested. We can too.

As much as it depends on you, stop doing everything you can:

- Everything unimportant.
- Everything compulsive or perfectionistic.
- Everything out of excessive fear.

Do not overpromise. Do not drift into *yes.* Sweep everything off the desk except that which will endure—and that which you are called to do. Everything else is for *somebody* else. Not for you.

Define what you want most—*and what you will want most later.* Rearrange the clock and calendar to support your core mission. Not every financial saving is worth the expense of time. Not every activity, however enjoyable, should make the cut.

Consider which activities you'll leave behind, just for now. This doesn't mean ruling out leisure and fun, which we all need, nor eliminating a day of Sabbath rest each week, as God requires. It does mean choosing with great intention from the array of shiny distractions beckoning for your attention every waking moment. You cannot do it all—so select those activities you treasure most.

Your Time and Energy Strategy

An effective shortcut to manage time is to manage energy. Factor an "energy strategy" into all scheduling.

Robert is a night owl with a day job. He schedules his highest concentration work for quiet evenings at his office. To avoid overwork, he often schedules a run in the park or other midday activities to get him out of the office and into sunlight.

Lori's creative energy peaks in the early morning. She rises before dawn and composes in sacred silence.

Christine is an introvert whose social resistance peaks in late afternoon. She schedules all important phone calls before four o'clock.

At what time of day are you most likely to fulfill—*or resist*—essential tasks? What predisposes you to peak performance—physically, creatively, and socially?

Are you affected by…sunlight? moonlight? hunger? hydration? You may be unable to change the ebb and flow of your body rhythms, but you can lean into them to enhance your productivity.

God owns time, and He wants us to pay attention to how we spend it. Rule your schedule like a kind, wise general, protecting your mission. *"Teach us to number our days, that we may gain a heart of wisdom,"* (Psalm 90:12).

Our call to greatness comes with a hidden expiration date. We have a window of opportunity to:

- exercise our passion
- courageously pursue our dreams
- make a Kingdom impact
- live a spiritually abundant life that blesses others

But at a preordained—and undisclosed—date, that window will close. Therefore, do only what is most important and necessary.

> For time to be anointed, it must first be appointed.
>
> Appoint your time wisely.

For time to be anointed, it must first be appointed.

Strategize Your Challenges: Outwit

Establish a mindset to outwit future obstacles with faith and creativity. Snags will arise. Handwringing is not in your playbook. Your strategy is to keep your wits about you—cool, calm, and ready to focus—not on despair, but on creative alternatives, possibilities, and scenarios.

The need to outwit problems never ceases. Your winning style is to maintain a demeanor of relaxed readiness. At a moment's notice, you'll switch gears and access waves of fresh creativity as you reconfigure options, rearrange priorities, and tweak old resources.

When the franchise company Guy represented announced the elimination of a core product line producing forty percent of agent revenues, many franchisees went into a well-deserved state of panic. Guy wasted no time lamenting what couldn't be changed. Instead, he sought to outthink, out-plan, and outwit the unsolvable—and by God's amazing grace, combined with Guy's faith and grit, he did it. He focused on every creative and imaginable possibility until his mind lighted on an alternate product, approved by the company but ignored by most because it was less profitable. He redirected all staff efforts to build that up as a replacement. Jobs were saved.

Always start with a cool head, a faith-driven heart, a relaxed, open, creatively disposed mind, and a blank page, screen, or graph. You can do this.

Strategize Your Staying Power: Outlast

As you work through your jigsaw puzzle strategy, you find a few extra pieces that don't seem to fit anywhere. By then, you've used up all your creative energy. You're tired. You want to give up. But don't.

When you've done all you know to do, that's the time to rely on your prayerful perseverance. Through perseverance, you really can outlast all your challenges.

Ted was a talented professional who'd recently formed a partnership to start up a business. He'd found the mission of his lifetime and was dedicated to doing the work he knew he was born to do. But shortly after the launch, his business partner changed his mind and wanted out. With no cash to buy out his partner's share and save his new business, Ted's only choice was to entangle himself in hopeless debt. The metrics estimated it would take twenty years to return Ted even to a net worth of zero. But he persevered—and prospered—in record time. By God's grace and mercy, Ted outlasted defeat. I can't disclose his net worth, but he is a success story for the ages.

Never give up, even when failure stares you in the face. Failure is not an ending point—it's a pause point. Pause and pray, regroup, and redirect your efforts. You may reach your dream later than hoped or in a different way than planned. But until God stops you, never give up.

Do you imagine the confident people you admire have never experienced failure? Hardly. They speak of failure in multiples, in plural terms, having passed through many valleys of loss and despair. But, by steadfast faith and unrelenting perseverance, they outlasted them all.

Diana put it this way: *"Sometimes, I see that jealous look in someone's eyes that scowls, 'Why do you have it—and I don't?' I want to put my arms around them to soothe their despair. I want to say, 'You're right. You do deserve it more than I do. You have more talent and ability than me. But you gave up. You stopped trying. You stopped showing up. I stayed in the game, counted the cost, prioritized time, refused to rest in my failures, and prayed for the courage and stamina to persevere to my finish line. I'm not better than you. I simply outlasted you."*

We all feel sadness for those who could have, would have, or should have.

Please don't let that person be you.

For personal reflection and discussion:

1. What is the most important aspect you learned about strategy?
2. In what way will you protect your boundaries?
3. In your enterprise, which extra puzzle piece needs placing?

Chapter Twelve

ENTREPRENEUR PLAYBOOK:
From Dream to Done, Part I

One of my great privileges as a financial advisor was observing numerous entrepreneurs navigate their journey from inspiration to realization of multi-million-dollar enterprises. Oh, how I rejoiced when they succeeded.

I carefully noted everything my clients did that worked—and what didn't. I've quantified twenty-three significant factors to help you succeed. These are not theories. They're case studies. I did not make them up. I wrote them down.

The factors that lead to entrepreneurial success are remarkably similar across many types of businesses. If you're frustrated by an aspect of your business plan that isn't working, I recommend you use the following two chapters as a diagnostic tool to help you pinpoint your business's precise area of weakness. It just might save your enterprise.

I was born to be an entrepreneur. I love business. Yet, I don't believe business ownership is for everybody. While it offers certain obvious advantages, self-employment makes excruciating demands on you that far exceed the legal demands of any employer.

God has wired each of us differently for His purposes. Our most direct path to financial confidence and wellness comes by following His lead.

If your calling is to be an entrepreneur, this practical, step-by-step playbook will prepare you for the journey. It's a proven model to take you from dream to done, instilling you with the confidence and readiness to succeed. *"The plans of the diligent lead to profit as surely as haste leads to poverty,"* (Proverbs 21:5).

Let's plan your strategy together…

DREAM Prayerfully

To make your business work, you'll need to incorporate higher thinking than is found in your own head. You'll need a God's-eye view of the landscape.

There are endlessly creative ways to do business—and more ways to fail than to succeed. Ask God to help you, guide you, and lead you. Be open to His will and His calling. If you're going to do this and make it work, seek counsel from your Silent Partner (who, incidentally, receives a 10% minimum off the top).

God knows His plans for your life and the roadblocks ahead. Dream prayerfully. This one step can save you twenty years. Don't skip it.

Dreaming takes guts, and few dare to do it. Many dream within a practical and narrow range, leaving no opening for miracles or breakthroughs. Some continue to work in robotic-like fashion on worn and burnt-out paths rather than daring to prayerfully dream something new.

Let the fear of failure go. Release its chokehold on your life. Get out of your own way, out of your own head, out of your own fears. Reach beyond space and time to capture your ideal calling, and do it now! Get it right this time. If you've already started on an off note, make a pivotal U-turn (and maybe save your life).

Why waste years of misdirected effort? You may already possess the essentials and need only a tweak or two. Dreaming prayerfully will capture God's Spirit—and awaken yours.

You may be a brilliant strategist. But logic alone, without the full engagement of the heart and spirit, may steer you to a place of regret. If you don't dream prayerfully, a part of you may later be repelled by the success you planned through logic alone. Don't leave God out of this critical step.

Dream prayerfully about the size of your dream and the tone, style, and manner in which you will intersect your gifts with the hungry world around you. Ask God which missing piece of the world's great puzzle you might honorably and profitably fill. Then, ask how He would have you fill it. This first step can save you decades of frustration and heartache. Don't skip it.

DEVOUR Counsel

To devour is to receive with gusto. One does not devour bitter medicine. Children devour lollipops, not Brussels sprouts. Devouring indicates enthusiasm and appreciation for what is being offered.

Many entrepreneurs make the mistake of depending on one tired person for counsel: themselves. You will likely have to execute alone, especially in the earliest days of your enterprise, perhaps without a team yet behind you.

But do not deliberate alone. Isolation is dangerous.

You need not fear counsel. As an entrepreneur, you are in charge. You don't have to execute anybody else's ideas except your own. But filter your ideas through wise counsel. Those ideas that remain standing will be well-developed, articulated, and strong. Receive and consider counsel with gusto.

DETERMINE Destination

Where are you headed? The world has set a default destination for your business. Don't let the winds of default carry it where you never wanted it to go. Business owners are faced with constant decision-making. How will you know if you should turn left or right if you do not know your destination?

To determine your destination, think ahead. What do you want your business to look like five years from now? Do you want to grow its revenues, expand its product line, or deepen its service offerings? Do you think you'll want to sell it?

By knowing your destination, you'll create a wise to-do list, focusing on issues including marketing, building a team, or assembling repeatable systems you describe in meticulous detail to make it possible for new hires—or future franchisees—to successfully duplicate your efforts. Be sure to determine in advance the destination for your profits. How will you use these to further God's Kingdom? What percentage will you give? At which points will you increase that percentage? What financial finish line would allow you to give it all away?

DESIGN Strategy

"Wishing" is not a strategy. You achieve very different results by design than by default. In business, "play it by ear" is playing to lose. Strategy structures a path to help you reach your full potential. Remember to think through and write out every minute detail of creating and delivering your product or service. In every enterprise, always remember...first, you choreograph. Then you dance.

DIFFERENTIATE Bravely

Who you are is so much more important than what you do. Even as a franchise owner or captive entrepreneur, the experience your customers have of working with or purchasing from you rather than another competitor is different. You bring something no one else has to the engagement: your authentic style.

> Your customers already know this. You may be the only one who does not know it.
>
> We do business with people we like.
>
> We like genuine people.

As clients and customers, we enjoy the unique personalities and quirky hobbies and interests of those with whom we do business. It makes us feel a warm and humanizing personal connection to them, and it gives us something to ask about when we meet.

So let *you* out of the bottle.

Like it or not, you already have a personal brand. Identify it. Ask everyone you know what they perceive to be your brand. What about you stands out to them? Lean intentionally into your natural style, manner, and inclinations. Build your entire business model around them. It will be instinctive and seem effortless.

Always be yourself. The brand called *you* offers a natural advantage no one else can effectively imitate. It's yours alone. Don't ignore it. Profit from it.

DESCRIBE Compellingly

Describe your unique value offering in a short, captivating way, and use that phrase or sentence all the time, everywhere, in printed materials, conversations, and in your social media presence.

It took me a long time to figure out this crucial missing link to my business development. But once I did, I went so far as to rename and rebrand my then well-established business from "Advantage Financial Planning" to "The Caring Advisor" to describe my unique value offering. Which of those two business names would you notice on a list?

You don't need to rename your business, of course, but you do need a tagline, theme, or catchy phrase that authentically describes and delights existing and potential customers.

If you're already in business, you may not realize what clients love most about doing business with you. Ask them. Invite your current customers to describe what they feel is your primary value to them. Their answers might surprise you. I spread a year's worth of client thank-you notes across my desk and found the word "caring" again and again. Bingo.

In a new business, describing your value very simply in a single phrase or sentence is even more critical. This attracts not only new customers but *the right customers,* those who are looking for your personality or style and will be most satisfied with you. Best of all, your descriptive phrase will give your existing customers words to use—talking points—to describe you when referring you to their friends.

One common mistake made by business leaders is to create complicated, clinical slogans that are factual, long-winded, or dreary. Describe who you are, what you do, and why you do it based on your *why*, not on your *how*. And if you can, make it fun.

DESIGNATE Support

No general can do it alone. You cannot lead in a vacuum. Success demands support. You'll have to choose the "who, what, when, and how" of support very carefully, according to a combination of logic, counsel, business planning, and brave gut instinct...but choose you must. And choose strategically. Take precise aim at *what* you are choosing to protect: your talent, energy, time, and profit.

Protect your talent.

You won't get from here to there running on the engine of someone else's talent. Your best hope for success is to exploit and deliver your unique talent to the world, the talent already bursting out of you, yearning to express itself but perhaps burdened by other business details that are not within your wheelhouse. Protect your unique talent from dilution and distress by finding other people to execute the miserable parts of your to-do list. God wired us differently. Your task of dilution is someone else's talent and dream. Give it to them. Let it go.

Protect your energy.

Think of a fine sports car deteriorating in rust. The world will not want what you create from an exhausted brain and body running on fumes. You may think you're hiding mental fatigue, but you're not. The world will pay for the best and brightest value you conceive and deliver through a highly sharpened, fit, and present mind and body. Designate support so that you can regenerate, recuperate, and reimagine.

Protect your time.

Your business does not own you. You own you. God owns you. As an entrepreneur, you did not offer to lay down your life as a soldier does in combat. Be clear about this. Protect your time. Offer carefully chosen others the opportunity to support you at the office, at the store, on the phone, or in the back room.

Protect your profit.

No matter your business model, the world will not pay you more to do it all yourself. Your only hope of achieving your profit potential is to leverage your time. If you want to generate more profit, pay for more support. Successful entrepreneurs hired support before you did, and they're reaching their goals in record time. You cannot deliver the best *you* unless you make room for *them* in your enterprise.

DEFINE Processes

If you're brave enough to be an entrepreneur, your most precious resource is time. You'll need to replicate the best of your value exponentially. There is only one way to do this: with defined processes others on your team can model.

Processes are all about safety and uniformity of outcome. Well-defined and smoothly executed processes assure your customers that their satisfying experience with your company will occur again if they refer their friends. If you go so far as to give a catchy name to your process, it will further add to your referrals by giving your clients talking points for their friends. Processes assure both you and your employees that they're doing the right job in the right way. Processes allow you or your management team efficient oversight of discrete tasks.

DIRECT Boldly

Every entrepreneur requires a particular type of moral courage that many find unpleasant. It's best to resolve this upfront because it never goes away.

To fulfill your mission, you will have to disappoint some people. It will hurt. They will survive. You cannot bring an employee mentality into self-employment. Fence-straddling has its place as a survival skill for employees of a large corporation. However, the skill set required to thrive as an entrepreneur differs vastly.

If you are called to lead, this is one fence you cannot straddle. Your employees, vendors, clients, and customers have hitched their needs to your wagon. You are the lead dog. Pray over your every decision and then direct boldly.

DO Imperfectly

The single most powerful business decision you can make is to will yourself to execute tasks before your impossible standards of perfectionism are satisfied.

You don't have time to get it right according to your superhuman standards. So get it done. You're in a war against failure. The troops of poverty are approaching. Don't wait another moment. Advance!

Whatever you do today will change tomorrow anyway. It will soon be shredded in yesterday's wastebasket of obsolescence. But the actions you take today will move you forward. And that's what you need to do. The world is full of bright people overflowing with talent but frozen in the false pride of perfectionism. Move forward. Resolve to be the headlights, not the deer.

The world is less likely to notice your imperfection and more likely to respond to your actions. Whatever you need to do to move toward your dream, do it today. Do it imperfectly.

Business failure doesn't usually happen in one single overwhelming event. Most entrepreneurs fail on the installment basis. Day after day of waiting for it to be just a little bit better.

Your perfectionism will not earn you the rewards you seek. Nobody is willing to pay enough for your distorted version of *perfect.* Do it. Do what you need to do. Do it now. Get up now and do it.

For personal reflection and discussion

1. Which action stands out to you as your priority?
2. In which area are you weakest? Strongest? Safest? Surest?
3. What new idea comes to mind for your business model? What step will you take to implement that idea?

Chapter Thirteen

ENTREPRENEUR PLAYBOOK: From Dream to Done, Part II

DELIVER Value

Delivering extreme value to your customers and clients does not just reflect your goodness—it reflects your brilliance.

Once you identify what your buyers value most and find a way to give it to them—abundantly and seamlessly—you'll eventually own your market share. Buyers will race to you, stay with you, and tell everyone they know about you. They'll be faithful despite your flaws, and flawless in their faith.

Value creation and award-winning delivery are the top secrets to entrepreneurial success. The mistake entrepreneurs make is in constructing how *they* will profit instead of constructing how their *customers* will profit.

Your business or product is not about you. It's about them.

Be passionate about profit—theirs.

DEIFY Only God

At some happy point, your business will be going well. Exceeding expectations. Blowing past your pro forma and surpassing your revenue goals. You've just won an award. Your photo appeared in a local journal, and your reputation is growing. Someone even asked you to speak at their event. My, you feel important.

The high point of your glory places you at terrifying risk of falling headlong into a low point of spiritual and financial impoverishment. When people exalt you—as they may well do when the noteworthy success you dreamed of becomes your reality, and your leadership reputation strengthens and expands—run hard to the Lord. Run fast. Bow low. Deify Him. Exalting God over self is the only way to safeguard your path from ruin.

Exalting God over self is the only way to safeguard your path from ruin.

DECIDE Daily

I know. You're not asking for much—just a bit more time to pause, ponder, and examine the facets of your decisions to be sure you decide correctly. After all, the stakes are high, and your cushion to absorb error is low.

But there's no time.

Those blasted requests for decisions rush at you like an avalanche of rocks and stones tumbling down a mountain. If only you could put on your helmet and walk away, but you can't. You're no longer an employee; you're an owner now. It's up to you to pick up each stone and decide. Quickly.

The larger rocks may allow you a few extra days of study, but all the little stones must be handled today.

Problems will not slow down and wait for you to resolve your indecision. It will not stop the problem from growing like a weed. Fear of failure may be excruciating—but indecision will paralyze your profit and potential.

Indecision may cause a troublesome tooth to become a root canal or a tangled tax matter to grow into a legal nightmare.

Here are some examples of potentially costly business indecision.

Whether to:

- Entice your team to greater productivity via a bonus plan—or risk losing talent by avoiding the increased expense.
- Ignore a client complaint because it's hard to deal with conflict—or resolve it before it turns into scathing litigation.
- Initiate a hard conversation with a disgruntled employee—or risk seeds of discontent taking root and overpowering the joy in your office.

The need for decision-making is unceasing. *And* this is what you signed up for. The rocks will keep tumbling. Catch them, juggle them, and learn to sort them quickly. Yes. No. Yes. No. Be a juggler. Decide daily.

What if you decide wrong? Take a breath. It will happen. Count on it. But if you've structured your business framework on biblical wisdom and truth, it will cushion minor slips in decision-making.

You're more likely to make the right choice, and when you don't, God will pick you up and help you recover.

DISPLAY Leadership

Leadership makes visible your calling, courage, commitment, and consistency to others. All leaders seek to develop these attributes, but great leaders *display* them continuously to their teams, colleagues, customers, and the world.

Your calling is your *why*. Be intentional about wearing your vision on your sleeve, with words ready to define your calling to anyone, anywhere, anytime. People who know *why* you are in business are more likely to emotionally connect with you and support your business.

Your courage is an attribute you may think is on sufficient display because you've willingly exchanged the security of a paycheck for the gut-wrenching uncertainty of starting a business and making a payroll. But others do not see that connection. They'll be on the lookout for your courage to be displayed by other means, such as how you respond when things go south or when emergencies occur. Though everyone will be afraid, be ready to comfort them with your bravery and thereby display your leadership.

Your commitment to your business must be absolute and inviolable, including a commitment…

- to your team, whom you will lead by trust and not by fear.
- to your customer's satisfaction, even knowing you'll be taken advantage of by a few.
- to paying your vendors on time.
- to honoring God by the way you interact with all others.

Your consistency demonstrates the seriousness and steadfastness of your promise and purpose. By consistency, you prove to every party associated with your business that they truly can depend on you.

DIGNIFY Relationships

One way you'll attract and keep safe the best and most loyal team, clients, customers, vendors, and family relationships, and keep them strong, is by overtly respecting every person you encounter. We all understand that no person we encounter is less important than we are, though they may have differing gifts, responsibilities, and assignments.

Unfortunately, no matter how much respect you offer, some, though they mean well, will disappoint. Others will violate your trust. Several employees may need to be dismissed from your firm. Even the best team member will require correction and refinement—in private. Along with frequent appreciation—in public.

Dignify every relationship, no matter how menial, trivial, or brief the encounter. Remember that there is no such thing as a *nobody* in God's kingdom. Ironically, each person's path is in a dynamic, fluid state. Yesterday's *nobody* may be tomorrow's *somebody*. Treat each person today like a *somebody* who's already earned their big promotion. And when they do, they'll remember you.

DETOXIFY Thinking

Business owners sometimes exhaust themselves by their own contorted rationale of the past, present, and future. As intelligent and good-hearted as you intend to be, you may be caught in a toxic loop circling beneath the radar of your consciousness.

As an entrepreneur seeking lasting success, you have no space to accommodate faulty thinking. Too much is at stake. You'll need to harness the precise weapon of clarity to navigate your complicated business landscape.

If you are embroiled in emotions and reactions you do not understand, don't waste precious time or profit playing loop-de-loop with toxicity. Pause and rethink the original, foundational intent of your entrepreneurial dream.

Compare that to your financial pain point. Is something from the past twisting or interfering with the reality of the present?

We all have a history. Thankfully, we also now have a relationship with the One who can heal it.

> Talk to the Lord.
>
> Talk to a counselor.
>
> Talk to yourself.
>
> Do not allow a damaged past to impact your future.

Create a brand-new loop to encircle your mind and emotions, one rooted in the truth of God's word—and nobody else's. You'll be amazed at how much energy is released when you break free of harmful thought patterns.

DEEPEN Capability

None of us can know the ceiling of God's plan for our lives. Wisely prepare for whatever opportunities He might send.

Ways we might deepen our capability…

- Broaden knowledge by joining a professional group.
- Earn an additional designation or degree.
- Expand the depth of your understanding by reading and studying.

- Devote yourself to practicing and refining a process or technique.
- Show up—being truly present—at continuing education classes.
- Make time to attend conferences, seminars, and retreats.

At the intersection of preparation and opportunity, we find wild opportunities and what appears to be "sudden" success—but you and I both know there was nothing sudden about it.

DETOUR Calmly

You just got word that your supplier has filed for bankruptcy before filling your already overdue order. The home company of which you are a franchisee has announced they will no longer offer the product that accounts for 40 percent of your revenues. A strange disease named COVID-19 is causing the entire country to stay home. Now what?

Detour calmly. The most precious tool in your emergency toolkit is your ability to think. Wild creativity cannot coexist with panic. When there's nothing you can do, there's always *something* you can do. Ask the Lord to open your mind and receive His direction. This is a time to be still and know that He is God (Psalm 46:10).

Wild creativity cannot coexist with panic.

Remember the old phrase, "Necessity is the mother of invention"? For you, as an entrepreneur, necessity is the mother of ***innovation.*** Innovation can expand your enterprise, skyrocket your profits, and make you wonder how you ever lived without it.

Take a breath or two. Detour calmly.

Then, innovate your way through your mountain.

DIVIDE Elephants

At some point, you'll either desire to take on an impossibly large challenge, or one may be handed to you. The size and scope of the elephant-sized project will overwhelm you—unless you divide your elephants into bite-size pieces.

Unless you invest the time to quantify and break down your project into tiny, manageable, and actionable units, the entirety of your challenge will freeze you into inaction or procrastination. Even fast-food chains divide the task of making a hamburger into twelve or more steps. Your project may require twelve hundred steps. Know what those steps are.

What bite-size action can you take to move the project forward? Do that.

DISMISS Failures

Notice the word is plural. Failures happen constantly to those of us who are courageously and actively pursuing dreams. Sometimes, a failure is small enough to call it a mistake. An easily correctable misstep. The wrong date on a social media post. The wrong price tag on a product. The wrong delivery to a customer.

Other times, the extent of your failure will render you speechless. You'll face a ten-rung drop from the ladder you worked so hard to climb. But climb it again, you will. It will go faster and smoother next time. You'll be infinitely smarter too.

Racking up these failures proves you're actively pursuing, trying, and growing. Regard them with curiosity. Fix them quickly and without emotion. Analyze them dispassionately, like a football coach watching game tape the day after a loss. Learn your lessons, and then dismiss them. Eyes on the road ahead.

Failure is not a part of your brand. It's a part of your education.

DWELL in Forgiveness

If you want to learn to practice forgiveness, by all means, go into business right away. You'll soon be confronted with outrageous affronts you never dreamed of.

Someone will lie to you.

Someone you helped most will appreciate you least.

Someone will undeservedly speak ill of you—or betray you.

As an entrepreneur, prepare to witness the worst in people, even those you formerly held in high esteem.

How will you handle all your justified grievances? God says you'll have to let them go.

Forgiveness is not letting them off the hook. It's handing the hook—and the spiritual heavy weight of its burden—to God, the only judge who can ultimately deal with their offense.

The benefits of your constant outflow of unconditional forgiveness will expand even beyond the spiritual. Dwelling in forgiveness as a state of mind fosters a countenance of upbeat cheer and relaxed happiness that counteracts the aging stress of business. Dwelling in forgiveness is like dwelling in the fun and freedom of youth while pursuing your dream.

DEFAULT to Optimism

Your business. Your life.

We can do this the easy way or the hard way.

The risks are so high. Wouldn't optimism be...unwise? Given what you know about your back office, stockroom, or unfulfilled orders, isn't optimism unwarranted?

No. Optimism doesn't harm you—it *shelters* you from carrying the unnecessary burden of downcast days. Radiating positivity and high expectations is a winning approach that attracts people like a magnet. We all want to feel that way. Lead us. Show us how.

Your facial expressions, the movements of your head and hands, and the exhale of your breath reveal what your words dare not say about your beliefs and expectations for your business. Your mood is infectious. In business, we call it a *culture.* And it is palpable.

Your countenance will cue your team, vendors, and customers whether to enjoy the experience of working with you—or to be on guard. To stand back—or to be *all in.*

An optimistic entrepreneur is surprised only when things go wrong—not when they go right. Profits and conflicts will come and go. You might as well have a good time on your journey.

DETACH Weekly

Drowning is a tragedy. And sometimes it happens without water.

You can drown in your business.

Without ordering yourself to take a weekly break to rest your tired arms from fighting against the raging current of work and stress, your weariness and burnout will eventually overtake you in an insurmountable wave of distress. Your dream will drown.

What has kept you from disconnecting for a day? Fear? Habit? Ego? A sense of urgency? Or maybe you don't know what else to do with your hours except work.

This is no way to live. Even God rested on the seventh day, and you can too. Yes, you can.

God explicitly orders a day of Sabbath worship and rest.

Play is a strategy of youth that reinvigorates body, mind, soul, and creativity.

Weekends are rightly famous for faith, family, and football.

Drowning would be a tragedy. You need a life vest. Why not thoroughly and utterly disconnect from your business at least weekly? Medical and psychiatric professionals' offices are full of those who don't.

For personal reflection and discussion:

1. Which action stands out as your priority?
2. In which area are you weakest? Strongest? Safest? Surest?
3. What new idea do you have for your business model?

Chapter Fourteen

THE PRINCIPLE OF WORDS: Expand Opportunities, Guard Relationships

Rocket Power

In the 1980s, I relished a rare opportunity to watch a NASA space launch with friends from a beach in St. Augustine, Florida, about a hundred miles south of Cape Canaveral. Seconds after lift-off, the spaceship Discovery roared across our vista in celestial wonder, overloading our senses. It shot into the heavens, shaking the sand beneath our feet. We were so awestruck by its thunder, strength, and speed that we burst into joyful tears. The experience lasted only seconds, but forty years later, its memory lives vividly in my senses. Joy like that never leaves you.

A few years later, I was thrilled to experience another launch. A colleague and I stood in a Tampa parking lot in happy anticipation, searching the sky for the Challenger liftoff. Trembling with joy, we held our breaths. Again came the thunder and strength that shook the pavement. In a surreal instant, an unsettling cloud formation twisted our senses to accept the unthinkable: the rocket had exploded.

Tears flowed in disbelief at the speed and power of overwhelming destruction. My chest still constricts whenever I recall that tragic moment.

Words are like that.

> Words race from our mouths like rockets.
>
> They produce happiness—or horror.
>
> Their power can be life-giving—or deadly.
>
> They may trigger tears of joy—or grief.
>
> Their emotional impact can last forever.

Your words will significantly impact your efforts, enterprise, and expansion. The deliberate use of words will help you optimize opportunities, open networks, and safeguard relationships from careless entrapment caused by rash, rude, or reckless words.

The Power of Words is *not* about "naming and claiming" anything, nor about misguided theology based on self-exaltation or foolish attempts to manipulate God. Neither is the Power of Words based on new-age positivity, which swiftly reverts to negativity when outcomes aren't so positive.

The Power of Words is in the Wisdom of Restraint

Our words have extraordinary power to make or break our happiness, confidence, and financial outcomes. They can attract—or wound—relationships, trust, and, ultimately, wealth. Through disciplined restraint, the Power of Words will strengthen any enterprise: a marriage, ministry, or financial mission.

The wise and intentional use of words will equip you to reach your potential. The upside of our words is unlimited. The downside is destruction.

Words are Assets

Chip is a good man who owns a small business. He has a deep knowledge of his industry and a genuine desire to do business honorably and justly. But Chip has a sharp tongue. Though his ethics are kind, his words are not. Rude and reckless words have cost him dearly in relationships. Nobody wants to do debate prep before engaging in conversation, but Chip's arrogant tone immediately puts others on the defensive—his sharp tongue cutting like a sword. *"The words of the reckless pierce like swords, but the tongue of the wise brings healing,"* (Proverbs 12:18).

Sandy is a corporate executive who ably controls a myriad of operations except one: she won't control her tongue. Her frequent outbursts expose annoyance, impatience, disrespect, and disregard for others. If Sandy is thinking it, Sandy is saying it. *"Whoever derides their neighbor has no sense, but the one who has understanding holds their tongue,"* (Proverbs 11:12). Reluctant colleagues politely tolerate her, but no one supports her. She has zero credibility.

Guy harnessed the Power of Words to build his business. By limiting his words to those reflecting humility, respect, and consideration for others, he never had to deal with broken relationships, even after times of intense conflict. This was a highly efficient process, freeing him to devote all his energies to breaking new ground, and never having to stop to perform relationship repair.

The Bible says humility comes before honor (Proverbs 15:33). Honor has indeed come to Guy. The respectful words he speaks to others—to all others, in all circumstances—are magnified in the words they return to him. His solid reputation is a form of riches. *"A good reputation is more valuable than costly perfume,"* (Ecclesiastes 7:1a, NLT).

Scripture is loaded with warnings about taming the tongue: *"But I tell you that everyone will have to give account on the day of judgment for every empty word they have spoken,"* (Matthew 12:36). It is costly to rebuild a house after a hurricane or tornado has demolished it. It's even costlier to rebuild a relationship after words have demolished it. And sometimes they are beyond repair. Some relationships cannot be rebuilt for any price.

Words are Currency

Words are currency offering a high return on investment. Through our kind, respectful words, we make deposits into others' lives. Careful, caring, and considerate words, such as *please, thank you, may I, I'm sorry,* and *forgive me,* are relational investments. These words pay us high-yield dividends through loyalty, advocacy, respect, and love. By speaking life into others, we inspire them to support our initiatives. From the fullness of their hearts and the enthusiasm of their referrals, they multiply our profits.

By contrast, rude or unkind words sharply reverse our return on investment. Our harsh words cause the withdrawal of a disproportionate amount of goodwill. Success is interrupted, relationships are strained, and momentum is paused. Besides losing the initial goodwill, we also forfeit all the dividends and interest we've accrued. Harsh words extract harsh penalties.

When relationships are shaky, confidence is compromised. We're forced to divert our energies to make up, clean up, and catch up. We're so busy fixing the old, we have no time to pursue the new. It becomes difficult to gain new ground. Never allow rude, rash, or recklessly spoken words to ruin what you're working so hard to build.

Words are treasures of great worth. *"The words of the godly are like sterling silver; the heart of a fool is worthless,"* (Proverbs 10:20, NLT). *"A word fitly spoken is like apples of gold in a setting of silver,"* (Proverbs 25:11, ESV). Like all treasures, they are costly to repair. And sometimes impossible to replace.

The Power of Words is an essential component of lasting success. Our every dream and pursuit will require the support of others. We are wise to engage in a godly manner and sustain harmonious relationships throughout all seasons, including storms of disagreement, dissension, and despair.

Words are Profitable

Disciplined words expand our enterprise. Our investment is nominal—but our ROI (return on investment) is phenomenal. Our life next year, next season, and next decade will be irrevocably impacted by the words we speak today.

Words expand our influence. *"One who has a pure heart and speaks with grace will have the king for a friend,"* (Proverbs 22:11). *"Through patience a ruler can be persuaded, and a gentle tongue can break a bone,"* (Proverbs 25:15). *"...sweetness of speech increases persuasiveness,"* (Proverbs 16:21b, NASB).

Words are Dangerous

Words launch from our tongues like missile-fired rockets. *"The tongue also is a fire, a world of evil among the parts of the body. It corrupts the whole body, sets the whole course of one's life on fire, and is itself set on fire by hell,"* (James 3:6).

The rude, rash, reckless words we fire at others can backfire and set *our own* relationships, dreams, and future endeavors ablaze. The Power of Words builds or destroys—it's up to us. Be intentional. Make words work for you, not against you. We must always direct our speech. The tongue must never be permitted to direct us.

Words are Forever

As a child, I learned the chorus, "Sticks and stones can break my bones, but words can never harm me." It's not true. Words certainly *can* harm me. Words *have* harmed me.

The impact of words often lasts a lifetime. The effects of a cruel word spoken to you in childhood may linger throughout your life. Unkind words are a speedy delivery system for heartache lasting decades.

Words are Seeds

Words are seeds, either of good or poisonous fruit. After planting, words take root in the hearts and minds of those who read or hear them. *"The soothing tongue is a tree of life, but a perverse tongue crushes the spirit,"* (Proverbs 15:4). Kind words are a tree of life, bearing fruit that heals, lifts, and restores. *"Gracious words are a honeycomb, sweet to the soul and healing to the bones,"* (Proverbs 16:24). Their impact can last a lifetime.

Many remember a word spoken to us even long ago that elevated our hopes and changed our lives. *"The mouth of the righteous is a fountain of life…"* (Proverbs 10:11). This kind of fountain never runs dry because its inspiration comes from God. We may never learn the true impact of our kind words this side of Heaven, but God knows. *"The LORD detests the thoughts of the wicked, but gracious words are pure in his sight,"* (Proverbs 15:26).

Unkind words are poisonous seeds bearing poisonous fruit. Some poisons we recognize immediately. Others release their toxins slowly over time, like specks of arsenic contaminating much-needed relationships so slowly, we may not even realize the damage that is happening. Their effect will show up later—as if suddenly.

> Rudeness fosters resentment.
>
> Rashness is fraught with unnecessary error.

Reckless speech lacks consideration for the other person. These harmful words disregard potential outcomes. Rude, rash, and reckless words are poisons you may not recognize initially as dangerous because their toxicity is hidden.

Words have the power of evil because they can twist opinions, reframe thinking, and reshape attitudes. That's why you must carefully guard the words you speak—and also the words you allow yourself to hear. Their well-hidden poison can destabilize a career, spoil a relationship, divide a family, or melt down a marriage.

Words are God's Weapons

God's words, spoken to us, over us, or by us, are fearsome weapons we can pray to break ties with our past and build our desired future. You can protect yourself from needless discouragement by speaking bold words of faith and Scripture into every situation.

When you are in trouble, God's words are mighty weapons of spiritual warfare (Ephesians 6:10-16). They are a way to safeguard your God-worth as defensive weapons to protect you from enemy assault, and offensive weapons for gaining new kingdom territory when pursuing a God-inspired goal.

Our words will always be imperfect, but God promises His word will not return to Him void.

Twelve Ways to Use Words with Wisdom and Restraint

1. When angry, place your thoughts in protective custody and do not release them until your emotions are under control.

   "A fool's mouth lashes out with pride, but the lips of the wise protect them," (Proverbs 14:3).

   "A gentle answer turns away wrath, but a harsh word stirs up anger," (Proverbs 15:1).

When angry, place your thoughts in protective custody and do not release them until your emotions are under control.

2. When rushed, do not be speed-trapped into making a rash promise.

   "Do you see someone who speaks in haste? There is more hope for a fool than for them," (Proverbs 29:20).

"Those who guard their lips preserve their lives, but those who speak rashly will come to ruin," (Proverbs 13:3).

3. When asked a question, do not interrupt.

    "To answer before listening—that is folly and shame," (Proverbs 18:13).

4. When seeking stress relief, do not succumb to rudeness.

    "Love is patient and kind; love does not envy or boast; it is not arrogant or rude. It does not insist on its own way; it is not irritable or resentful…" (1 Corinthians 13:4-6, ESV).

    "Do not let any unwholesome talk come out of your mouths, but only what is helpful for building others up according to their needs, that it may benefit those who listen," (Ephesians 4:29).

5. When you must impress, do not overpromise.

    "Like clouds and wind without rain is a man who boasts of a gift he does not give," (Proverbs 25:14, ESV).

6. When tempted to flattery or insincerity, do not say another word or your future words will be suspect.

    "A lying tongue hates those it hurts, and a flattering mouth works ruin," (Proverbs 26:28).

7. When wrong, accept criticism with gracious dignity.

    "The wise are glad to be instructed, but babbling fools fall flat on their faces," (Proverbs 10:8, NLT).

8. When in a dispute, abstain from slander.

    "Without wood a fire goes out; without a gossip a quarrel dies down," (Proverbs 26:20). "

A gossip betrays a confidence, but a trustworthy person keeps a secret," (Proverbs 11:13).

9. When in a threatening situation, don't worsen it.

   "Those who guard their mouths and their tongues keep themselves from calamity," (Proverbs 21:23).

10. When feeling sarcastic, you won't need to bite your tongue if there's no ill will hiding in your heart.

    "For the mouth speaks what the heart is full of," (Luke 6:45b).

11. When serving those for whom you care, use your words. Though there are things a client does not know about you, the fact that you care must never be one of them.

    "Love one another with brotherly affection. Outdo one another in showing honor," (Romans 12:10, ESV).

12. When you want to clean up your words, clean up your heart.

    "For out of the overflow of the heart, the mouth speaks," (Luke 6:45a, BSB).

Expand Opportunities, Guard Relationships

Words have the power to construct, obstruct, or destruct.

Bridle your words, and you'll bundle your profits—spiritually, emotionally, relationally, and financially.

"Death and life are in the power of the tongue…" (Proverbs 18:21a, ESV).

Words hold power. Make that power yours.

For personal reflection and discussion:

1. Is there someone in your life with whom identity repair is needed? What will you do about it?
2. Can you recall words that have significantly impacted or changed your life, for better or for worse?
3. How do you plan to use the Power of Words to upgrade your life and equip you for success?

Chapter Fifteen

BUILDING WORD MUSCLES: Learn How to Talk Back

As we seek to develop our full financial potential, you and I have an enemy whose mission is to deceive us about who God created us to be. Cunning and persuasive, the enemy whispers accusations and lies into our minds in our weakest moments. If he can unravel us at our roots, he can foil God's good plan for our lives. His mission is to rob us of the blessing we might bring to others if we were financially whole and strong.

As children, we were taught not to talk back. However, as Christian warriors fighting this invisible enemy, we must talk back—loudly and firmly.

Speaking and agreeing with God's word about who you are in Christ is a powerful weapon against discouragement and defeat. We must learn to trade self-talk for God-talk.

"We demolish arguments and every pretension that sets itself up against the knowledge of God, and we take captive every thought to make it obedient to Christ," (2 Corinthians 10:5). Speak God's words daily as your shield to defend your dreams. Speak truth *to* yourself, *over* yourself, every day. This is not self-talk; it's God-talk.

Your Handy Identity Protection Company

A man called an identity protection company.

"I want to protect my identity," he said.

"What is your name?" they asked.

"I'm not sure," he replied. "I don't really know who I am."

Click.

The identity protection company hung up.

Until we define our identity, we'll have a tough time protecting it. We must continually remind ourselves who we are in Christ—not who we used to be before coming to faith. Your *old self* may sometimes stalk you—but it is no longer the *real* you.

Jack Learned the Truth

After a painful childhood, Jack's identity was riddled with untruths:

- He *told himself* he was unloved—but Jack was dearly loved by God himself.
- He *told himself* his broken childhood sentenced him to permanent brokenness—but God had ordained a fabulous future for Jack.
- He *told himself* he was alone—but Jack was attentively watched day and night by God's security force.
- He *told himself* he was a pauper—but Jack was an heir to the King of Kings.
- He *told himself* he had insufficient connections to forge a viable success path—but Jack was well-connected to the One who *created* everything, *owns* everything, and can maneuver Jack *through* anything.

Define Yourself as God Does

Many of us unconsciously recirculate toxic thoughts about ourselves that appear logical based on our history or past. But if they deny the unabashed, cleansing love of the Father, they are falsehoods. God's beautiful intention for our future may be downright illogical—but it is blessedly true. *"'For I know the plans I have for you,' declares the* L*ORD, 'Plans to prosper you and not to harm you, plans to give you hope and a future,'"* (Jeremiah 29:11).

While we'll never perfectly embody all God has for us while we sojourn on earth, we can learn to defend ourselves against the disheartening deceit of the enemy. Jack accepted falsehoods without a fight. Remedial identity repair was necessary for him to build a spiritually rich and abundant life in a fallen world. Thankfully, he did.

Like Jack, we need to remind ourselves, through Scripture, who God made us to be in Christ—not who past circumstances diverted us to be for a time. Make all new decisions from your holy imagination rather than from your unholy past.

Fix your gaze heavenward, and set your soul's GPS toward the completed state through which our merciful God chooses to see you because of His Son. Only then will you be able to lessen the raging tug of war between your best and worst self. Only then will your actions be congruent with your intentions.

Shut down the noise and confusion. Always be mindful of your identity in Christ.

Learn to Talk Back

One way we talk back to untruths is via word prompts. A prompt is a cue, a reminder, to supply us with a forgotten word. Merriam-Webster says a prompt "assists by suggesting or saying the next words of something forgotten or imperfectly learned."[3]

Why create word prompts? Because there are already negative prompts in our minds that cue us many times each day. For the future we want to build, we need to replace disempowering falsehood with empowering truth. Not damaged, inflated, historical, experiential, secular, or relational truth, but God's truth about who He made us to be. The astonishing power of God's word is a weapon and shield that will defend our dreams—and secure our destiny.

I recommend you carry a handful of word prompts with you every day. Never be without your truths. When a pain point stabs without warning, there's no time to hunt for your favorite Scriptures. You need them boxed and ready to go.

"Be alert and of sober mind. Your enemy the devil prowls around like a roaring lion looking for someone to devour," (1 Peter 5:8).

Use your word prompts as a preemptive strike before…

- your follow-up meeting with your biggest client.
- your interview at the university you've dreamed of attending since sixth grade.
- your first step onto the podium before you take the microphone.

3 "prompt." Merriam-Webster.com. November 8, 2024. https://www.merriam-webster.com/dictionary/prompt.

16 Truths

Here are sixteen invaluable word prompts: Scriptures that replenish truths about who you are in Christ so your new self can always be ready to talk back to your *old self*. You can trust that what the Word of God says about you is truth. His word will not return void (Isaiah 55:11, AMPC).

In alphabetical order, for ease of future reference…

I am Calm.

"Cast all your anxiety on him because he cares for you," (1 Peter 5:7).

"Do not be anxious about anything, but in every situation, by prayer and petition, with thanksgiving, present your requests to God," (Philippians 4:6).

"He says, 'Be still, and know that I am God; I will be exalted among the nations, I will be exalted in the earth," (Psalm 46:10).

I am Cheerful.

"A cheerful heart is good medicine, but a broken spirit saps a person's strength," (Proverbs 17:22, NLT).

"'These things I have spoken to you so that in Me you may have peace. In the world you will have tribulation; but be of good cheer, I have overcome the world,'" (John 16:33, NKJV).

I am Content.

"But godliness with contentment is great gain," (1 Timothy 6:6).

"Then he said to them, 'Watch out! Be on your guard against all kinds of greed; life does not consist in an abundance of possessions,'" (Luke 12:15).

"Keep your lives free from the love of money and be content with what you have, because God has said, 'Never will I leave you; never will I forsake you,'" (Hebrews 13:5).

I am Courageous.

"The LORD is my light and my salvation; whom shall I fear? The LORD is the stronghold of my life; of whom shall I be afraid?" (Psalm 27:1, ESV).

"For God has not given us a spirit of fear and timidity, but of power, love, and self-discipline," (2 Timothy 1:7, NLT).

"Fear of man will prove to be a snare, but whoever trusts in the LORD is kept safe," (Proverbs 29:25).

I am Disciplined.

"Whatever you do, do your work heartily, as for the Lord and not for people, knowing that it is from the Lord that you will receive the reward of the inheritance. It is the Lord Christ whom you serve," (Colossians 3:23-24, NASB).

"Above all else, guard your affections. For they influence everything else in your life," (Proverbs 4:23, TLB).

I am God's Child.

"See how very much our Father loves us, for he calls us his children, and that is what we are! But the people who belong to this world don't recognize that we are God's children because they don't know him," (1 John 3:1, NLT).

"Even if my father and my mother abandon me, the LORD will hold me close," (Psalm 27:10, NLT).

I am Kind.

"Your own soul is nourished when you are kind; it is destroyed when you are cruel," (Proverbs 11:17, TLB).

"Whoever oppresses the poor shows contempt for their Maker, but whoever is kind to the needy honors God," (Proverbs 14:31).

"The King will reply, 'Truly I tell you, whatever you did for one of the least of these brothers and sisters of mine, you did for me,'" (Matthew 25:40).

I am Patient.

"A person's discretion makes him slow to anger, And it is his glory to overlook an offense," (Proverbs 19:11, NASB).

"Love is patient and kind; love does not envy or boast; it is not arrogant or rude. It does not insist on its own way; it is not irritable or resentful," (1 Corinthians 13:4-5, ESV).

I am Peaceful.

"A calm and peaceful and tranquil heart is life and health to the body, But passion and envy are like rottenness to the bones," (Proverbs 14:30, AMP).

"You will keep in perfect peace those whose minds are steadfast, because they trust in you," (Isaiah 26:3).

"Peace I leave with you; my peace I give you. I do not give to you as the world gives. Do not let your hearts be troubled and do not be afraid," (John 14:27).

I am Present.

"This is the day the LORD has made. We will rejoice and be glad in it," (Psalm 118:24, NLT).

"Therefore do not worry about tomorrow, for tomorrow will worry about itself. Each day has enough trouble of its own," (Matthew 6:34).

I am Restful.

"In peace I will lie down and sleep, for you alone, O LORD, will keep me safe," (Psalm 4:8, NLT).

"In vain you rise early and stay up late, toiling for food to eat—for he grants sleep to those he loves," (Psalm 127:2).

"'Come to me, all you who are weary and burdened, and I will give you rest,'" (Matthew 11:28).

I am Safe.

"The name of the LORD is a strong tower; The righteous runs into it and is safe," (Proverbs 18:10, NASB).

"Every word of God is flawless; he is a shield to those who take refuge in him," (Proverbs 30:5).

"So do not fear, for I am with you; do not be dismayed, for I am your God. I will strengthen you and help you; I will uphold you with my righteous right hand," (Isaiah 41:10).

I am Strong.

"Finally, be strong in the Lord and in his mighty power," (Ephesians 6:10).

"The LORD is my strength and my shield; my heart trusts in him, and he helps me. My heart leaps for joy, and with my song I praise him," (Psalm 28:7).

"I can do all this through him who gives me strength," (Philippians 4:13).

I am Thankful.

"...give thanks in all circumstances; for this is God's will for you in Christ Jesus," (1 Thessalonians 5:18).

"I will give thanks to the LORD because of his righteousness; I will sing the praises of the name of the LORD Most High," (Psalm 7:17).

I am Unique.

"For you created my inmost being; you knit me together in my mother's womb. I praise you because I am fearfully and wonderfully made; your works are wonderful, I know that full well...Your eyes saw my unformed body; all the days ordained for me were written in your book before one of them came to be," (Psalm 139:13-14, 16).

"Do not copy the behavior and customs of this world, but let God transform you into a new person by changing the way you think. Then you will learn to know God's will for you, which is good and pleasing and perfect," (Romans 12:2, NLT).

I am Victorious.

"Brothers and sisters, I do not regard myself as having taken hold of it yet; but one thing I do: forgetting what lies behind and reaching forward to what lies ahead, I press on toward the goal for the prize of the upward call of God in Christ Jesus," (Philippians 3:13-14, NASB).

"For I am confident of this very thing, that He who began a good work among you will complete it by the day of Christ Jesus," (Philippians 1:6, NASB).

"For the LORD your God is the one who goes with you to fight for you against your enemies to give you victory," (Deuteronomy 20:4).

With Scriptures in hand, you're ready. You've buckled up with truth—so step out in confident faith.

May God's word guard your mind, your tongue, and your outcomes.

For personal reflection and discussion:

1. What is your most vulnerable area to protect from deceit?
2. What have you told yourself about yourself that just isn't true?
3. Which Scriptures will you depend on to combat the enemy's lies with God's truth?

Chapter Sixteen

THE PRINCIPLE OF PRAYER:
Who Do You Know?

You may have seen the iconic 1963 photo of President John F. Kennedy working in the Oval Office as his 3-year-old son, John-John, played happily underneath his father's desk. What a beautiful and unforgettable image. Little John-John and his sister, Caroline, were too young to comprehend the unbelievable advantage of having a father who possessed such great power. Yet their advantage was nothing compared to ours.

Our God is not a U.S. President.

He is not the leader of the free world.

He's the leader of the *whole* world.

And you and I are His children who get to play under His desk.

"But as many as received Him, to them He gave the right to become children of God, to those who believe in His name, who were born, not of blood, nor of the will of the flesh, nor of the will of a man, but of God," (John 1:12-13, NASB).

I find it an astonishing privilege that through the blood of Jesus, God regards Himself as our Father, refers to us as His children, and grants us unlimited opportunities to talk with Him.

This is the thunderous Power of Prayer.

Access is a matter of who you know. Thankfully, we know Him. Think, for a moment, of the magnitude of this opportunity. If we requested personal access to a U.S. President, we'd likely be denied.

Presidents are elected *by* us but are protected *from* us. Only their own children get to play at their desks.

Presidents have no time to listen to our troubles. They're carefully shielded from interruptions. Even if we're suffering a heavy burden or an urgent injustice and desperately need to talk, our only option is to write a letter—a letter unlikely to be read.

And it's not just presidents who limit our access.

A few years ago, friends of mine were thrilled to be granted an appointment to discuss a serious matter with a U.S. Senator. They were given all kinds of instructions and told they'd have ten minutes to present their case. My friends feared that if, in nervous excitement, they forgot to make an important point, there'd be no opportunity for a second visit. You can imagine how carefully they planned and rehearsed to say exactly the right words before their clock ran out.

A Child's Advantage

Through Jesus, we can contact the Lord in prayer, day or night. Unlike my friend's appointment with the senator, no planning or rehearsals are necessary.

We don't have to finish in ten minutes.

The clock is *not* ticking.

If we forget to tell Him something, we can return and whisper it later.

We can freely approach Him at any time, for any reason, as often as we wish.

His counsel is free for those with faith in Him. No hourly cost. No bill. Jesus prepaid it.

We're not bound by a dress code or requirement to use pious-sounding words. We can laugh, cry, ask, beg, or ramble like a three-year-old child, for He is our Father.

We can take as much time as we want to define our dreams, express our fears, describe our troubles, plead our case, and ask for His guidance, direction, mercy, or rescue.

Who would willingly give up an opportunity like this?

Kings and princes have access to the best mentoring and counsel.

Through the extraordinary Power of Prayer, so do we.

Imagine being coached by God Himself, the One who knows all the players in your wealth story and who owns all the assets in the world. He has the power to rearrange any circumstance He chooses. Access to this kind of power is not found anywhere but in Him.

The magnitude of this privilege astounds me. As a business owner, it gave me an almost ridiculous advantage. I've long wondered why more dreamers, while pursuing their dreams, don't pursue the Power of Prayer.

18 Distinct Privileges of Prayer

1. Prayer reminds us that we are known, heard, and loved by God. As we deepen that relationship, we find bold courage to take on significant and meaningful challenges, trusting His holy safety net to hover over our initiatives.
2. Prayer regenerates much-needed faith. When financial circumstances are dire or a business opportunity gets sidelined, prayer increases our trust that God can circumvent financial disaster and open a new door. This renews our faith to push past adversity toward our goals.
3. Prayer is how we take heavenly "legal" action against another. When we have been wronged, we can make our case before God. In this way, we can fight for what seems right without breaking relationships.
4. Prayer provides us an opportunity to listen for God's voice. He speaks to us through the Holy Spirit and Scripture (Romans 8:26). His truths are empowering. He invites us to listen.
5. Prayer recalibrates our anxious hearts when we're distressed by uncertainties. We cast our anxieties on Him, knowing He cares for us affectionately and watchfully.
6. Prayer is how we keep our sanity when the world seems to have gone crazy. Reminding ourselves that nothing takes Him by surprise, we learn to filter everyday business interactions and financial events through His divine lens.

7. Prayer offers immediate response times when we need to report a problem to the One in power. We're never asked to wait six weeks for the next available *prayer appointment.* We're never forced onto a waiting list to reserve God's ear. He's never out of town, out of reach, or out of access when we, His children, need Him.
8. Prayer is therapy for the maladies of humanity. When we're disappointed with clients, vendors, colleagues, or ourselves, we can express our disappointments directly to the Lord. He helps us release anger, forgive others, get unstuck, and move forward. He invites us to seek His forgiveness for our own failings—and does so without cruel condemnation, but with a Father's love.
9. Prayer is private. This is a crucial need for business leaders. What you can tell no one else, you can tell God. Prayer is 100 percent secure, encrypted, and without risk. He is in your corner and will be faithful to keep your sacred trust. Communication with Him eases the loneliness that so often accompanies leadership.
10. Prayer cleans out dusty drawers of forgotten sin interfering with our upward progress. As we prayerfully journey our way toward our dream, we suddenly recall a matter that needs God's cleansing. Without pausing to make it right with God, we'd attempt to build a towering structure of success on a weak foundation. Prayer provides support beams to undergird the structural integrity of our path.
11. Prayer awakens us at the deepest level. It's the world's best wake-up call. We'd be at such a disadvantage to sleepwalk through life and miss miraculous moments of divine intervention, including whispered warnings that save us from sorrow or regret.

12. Prayer settles spiritual indigestion. It's antacid for the soul. Some things this side of Heaven will never be made right. Through prayer, we ask God's grace to digest the insufferable realities of this fallen world, even as we try to overcome them.

13. Prayer fills us up. Some mornings, we think we're not hungry for prayer—until we start *tasting it*. Yum.

14. Prayer is a remedy for robotic living. A day without prayer feels noisy and headachy. A week without prayer stirs stress akin to spiritual low blood sugar. A life without prayer is like living in a spiritual coma.

15. Prayer is fertilizer. It grows our love for unlovable others—a highly useful tool when building a wealth-confident life, certain to be populated by at least a few people not of our choosing. Through prayer, we begin to feel and sense His love for that difficult person. Over time, we can grow in genuine tenderness for many difficult people if only we will pray for them.

16. Prayer overcomes the deep hurt of being misunderstood. Though clients, colleagues, and competitors may sometimes misunderstand our kindest, sincerest efforts, God never misunderstands us (see Hebrews 4:12). Our Perfect Father always recognizes the truth of our intentions.

17. Prayer is a mountaintop experience—even for non-athletes. It generates exhilaration that invigorates our best efforts and inspires our most productive days.

18. Prayer turns on a light that overpowers darkness. If enough of us pray, we can light up a whole country. *If enough of us pray, we can light the whole earth* (2 Chronicles 7:14).

How Should I Pray?

If it's been a while since you've set aside time for intimate prayer over your dreams for your life, *that time is now*. This is a holy conversation worth having—even if you stammer your way through at first.

Prayer is the purest communication in the world. An intimate conversation between you and God. Before praying, we're not asked to clean up our act, our mindset, or our sentence structure. Rather, it's often intense and personal, raw and uncensored, a disorganized outpouring of unfiltered thoughts and emotions.

God loves us with a Father's love and is highly invested in our outcome. *"I will instruct you and teach you in the way you should go; I will counsel you with my loving eye on you,"* (Psalm 32:8). Don't miss the Power of Prayer. You can trust God. Your words will be private. A good, good Father with a treasured child alone together. What could be more precious than that?

How Prayer Builds Wealth Confidence

Praying is different from wishing, hoping, fretting, worrying, or positive thinking. These should never be confused with prayer. Prayer is an actual conversation with a living God.

In prayer, we can freely share with Him, among other things, every precious detail of our fantastic dream, our fervent desire for godly success, and our ferocious struggle to resist defeat.

We can ask Him…

- For wisdom in making critical business decisions.
- For help in increasing a skill set or developing an ability or talent.

- For strength to let go of something—or someone.
- For forgiveness over mistakes and blunders you've made along the way.
- For Him to grant you the favor of someone making decisions that will impact you.
- For doors to open where, at present, none are visible.
- For funds you need to provide for yourself and your family.
- For Him to reveal His will regarding the direction of your financial path.

"For we do not have a high priest who is unable to empathize with our weaknesses, but we have one who has been tempted in every way, just as we are—yet he did not sin. Let us then approach God's throne of grace with confidence, so that we may receive mercy and find grace to help us in our time of need," (Hebrews 4:15-16).

Invite God into your wealth story. Ask Him to mentor you to success, whatever that looks like in His ordained design for you. He is highly invested in your future. His way will be the best way.

For personal reflection and discussion:

1. What is one thing you'd like to talk to God about?
2. How will you benefit by establishing an active prayer time?
3. How might developing an active prayer life build your wealth-confidence?

Chapter Seventeen

LIVING IN THE POWER OF SEVEN

Marcy was a hard-working professional, a wonderful woman who loved God, her job, and other people. Her excellent efforts awarded her a six-figure promotion and a thirty-thousand-dollar bonus. What a boon to this single woman in her mid-fifties.

However, the bonus presented a problem: Marcy believed wealth was sinful. Though God had equipped her with a talent for earning, Marcy was uncomfortable with success. Her mindset prevented her from seeing God's hand in her finances, never occurring to her that He had given her an opportunity to glorify Him with extreme Kingdom generosity.

Though she was wise not to *love* money, she forfeited the chance to *use* money for God's purposes. Unsettled by financial success, she made no plan for it. All she thought to do at that moment was get the money out of her hands—fast.

She impulsively handed her entire bonus to her deadbeat brother-in-law, hoping to help him do better. He predictably squandered it on sinful behavior.

Marcy had a long history of undermining wealth. Her financial identity rested on holding herself down low. To her, an increase in wealth meant a decrease in honor. Poverty proved humility. Affluence proved arrogance. Or so she believed.

What a tight squeeze for a worker whose career was deservedly on the rise. It was illogical, but as she ascended in the ranks, she suffered from imposter syndrome. God had given her the ability to produce wealth (Deuteronomy 8:18), yet she preferred to see herself as a pauper—not the financial leader He had ordained her to be. Sadly, she wasted countless opportunities to make a financial impact for the Kingdom of God.

Do You Attract Or Repel Wealth?

Why would someone waste their chance to make a financial impact? Often, it's to protect the perceived truth of their financial identity. They define themselves by a certain wealth level and unconsciously hold themselves to the false "truth" of that label.

If you believe your financial identity is poor, you'll always find ways to decrease wealth no matter how much money God sends your way. Even if you earn or receive a great sum, you'll find a way to rid yourself of it so you can return to your authentic and comfortable identity of being poor.

I've seen it many times throughout the years. The ramifications are broad, spanning every aspect of our lives.

From a flawed financial identity, we may accidentally choose...

The wrong friends.

The wrong career.

The wrong spouse.

The wrong solution.

The wrong life.

How can you tell if your financial identity is poor? Simple. Ask yourself one question: In the past, when you've received a large sum, have you always spent it? That is your answer.

Are You Living a *Less-Than* Life?

It is frustrating to watch lovely people living *less-than* lives, wondering why their dreams aren't materializing, not pursuing the passion stirring their hearts because they don't realize Who is doing the stirring.

It is grievous to see dear, hopeful ones, full of talent, bursting with potential, frozen in fear, not daring to pursue any dream at all.

I hate to see Christians fail. And you don't have to. Hiding is not holiness. You don't have to live passively to please God. Does a lesser financial life prove a greater devotion to Him? I think not. The surefooted Christian striving in faith models far more trust in God than the frozen one shrinking in fear. If your lifestyle is grounded in God's word, you can live nobly and well at almost any financial level.

Ask the Lord, through the truth of His word, to resolve your financial identity and intention. If you are rooted in God's word, you'll find ways to build a purpose-driven future that will glorify Him. No matter your present financial state, you'll exude holy confidence and unhindered drive to press toward big dreams. And you'll live in the fullness of God's dream for you.

Ask the Lord, through the truth of His word, to resolve your financial identity and intention.

What's the point of living a powerless life? *Powerless* is not a synonym for *holiness*. Why tiptoe through your tomorrows? Isn't life hard enough? The Lord wants us to get it right and be empowered from within to initiate and innovate worthy pursuits in grand financial style—for His glory.

God owns all the money in the world. It is safe to allow some of His funds to flow through our hands if we use them to glorify Him through radical generosity. Impoverishment is not the only holy position.

God has chosen you to be productive for *His* sake. And that is not too much for you because He has pre-wired you for service. Remember, you have come into this world factory pre-wired (Psalm 139:13-16).

Point your compass toward the Lord—before, during, and especially after attaining success. Build your financial structure around *His* ownership and *your* stewardship of His resources, and you can freely pursue the dream in your heart without leaving your faith behind. You can serve the Lord with wholehearted confidence, the kind that powers through obstacles and reaches high to touch whatever dream of success He's ordained for your life. *"In the reverent* and *worshipful fear of the Lord there is strong confidence…"* (Proverbs 14:26, AMPC).

Seven Tutors

The Power of Seven is a simplified delivery system to fill your fearful tank with godly financial confidence. These proven principles are like seven tutors who coach you with important truths to sustain you to your financial finish line.

The result? Authentic, organic, godly financial confidence propelling you to create and enact your dream, infused with inside-out strength and staying power to support you in every season and chapter of your amazing life.

Embrace the opportunities He lays before you. Cast down fear, knowing your goal isn't selfish gain but Kingdom glory. As a Christ-follower, you long to pursue great and noble paths so you can:

- Run the race toward heaven-inspired goals (Hebrews 12:1).
- Offer yourself to others, pressing forward, not shrinking back, confidently inviting new relationships and circumstances into your ever-increasing fold (2 Timothy 1:7).
- Walk with lightness in your step and depth in your spirit (Proverbs 3:23).
- Model with authenticity the vibrant life of a much-loved child of the risen Lord (Psalm 139:13-18).
- Defy the odds and move beyond your childhood sorrow or disadvantage to remarkable and praiseworthy advantage (Genesis 50:20).
- Accomplish far more in your lifetime than you'd dare to dream or imagine (Ephesians 3:20).

Fifty Years of Power

I've known the man who inspired *Wealth-Confident* for fifty years and counting.

In his fifties, he "lost it all," financially speaking, and had to start over. His business was nearly destroyed, but by God's grace, he saved it.

In his sixties, he multiplied his business five times over.

In his seventies, a corporate decision beyond his control cost him half his accounts and income. Yet he never lost his cheerful outlook—*not ever.* He used that excruciating financial season to strengthen his muscles of generosity.

In his eighties, he's going strong, at the head of the pack, vigorously applying resilience, focus, discipline, forgiveness, and prayer every single day.

He's confident in this day and confident in the hope of tomorrow. God is his confidence (Proverbs 3:26).

Guy's Tool Chest

1. He knows who he is in Christ and is confident in his identity.
2. He defines his mission and knows exactly what he is trying to do.
3. He gives himself permission to commit.
4. He proceeds with excellence.
5. He creates a strategy for each mission and never gives up.
6. He is disciplined and intentional in his words.
7. He listens for the Lord's direction through prayer.

Your Swiss Army Knife—for Success

The Power of Seven is a multi-faceted tool that cuts through roadblocks rising against you, fitting perfectly in your faith walk. Tuck them into your planning, and pull them out when you need…

- **An Inspiring Tool**
  The Power of Seven will open your mind to dreams you've never considered. They'll inspire you to reach for and capture godly success.

- **A Spiritual Tool**
  They'll remind you of biblical truths and principles of the godly life that feed—or starve—financial confidence.

- **A Diagnostic Tool**
  When you struggle, they'll assess what's working for you—and against you.
- **A Protective Tool**
  They'll reveal the potential ambush hiding in the bushes, ready to trip you up if not addressed.
- **A Refining Tool**
  They'll help you smooth the edges of impulse and instinct into a noble and elegant financial pattern that satisfies you—and glorifies God.
- **A Sustaining Tool**
  They'll steadfastly escort you toward your future, soothe you on your worst days, and keep you from turning back when the road gets hard.

Is Your Dream in Hiding?

In the first chapter, we met Victoria and her siblings. You now understand why she thrived while her siblings struggled. Their struggle was not due to a lack of talent or earnest desire, but only to a shortfall of actionable power. Since they've implemented the Power of Seven, they are now reaching for the fullness of their potential.

Victoria was well on her confident way, but now, an exciting new dream has come into focus. A new mission has emerged that will build on the talents, skills, and experience she developed in her previous enterprise. She is gleeful.

Perhaps your dream is still in hiding. How frustrating! We've all met that rare individual who knew what they wanted to do with their life by sixth grade. They seemed so sure, confident, and self-directed. You fear your own dream may never show itself at all.

No need for dismay. Dreams present themselves in different ways. Stay on the lookout, and above all, stay alert.

Some dreams are gentle. If you listen for His whisper, you will at some point feel a stirring within you, like a scarf moved by a light breeze. You may feel the sway of awakening, a curiosity about something you hadn't considered before. Sit with this for a while, pray, and observe if the idea swells or passes. It may be fleeting. Or God may be stirring you with His ordained plan for your life.

Some dreams are withheld for a time by our Perfect Parent in Heaven. You've not been permitted to discover those dreams quite yet. You're just not ready. If you've been waiting a long time, you may fear God has forgotten you. He hasn't. Your ordained life is not like a restaurant doggie bag, shoved to the back of the refrigerator, forgotten and spoiling. No one escapes God's loving view. Your life is on purpose—for His purpose. Trust Him. Stay close. Be sure to faithfully execute what is in front of you, though it may not be ideal. He is keeping track. Prayerfully take each next step. Stay alert. Pray always.

Some dreams hide in plain sight. They are already in front of you, but you cannot see them yet. The mist is there for His reason. He will lift it in His timing,

and then your dream will come into exquisite focus. Your "aha" moment is coming. In the meantime, prepare yourself to be equipped and ready to go whenever God reveals it. Keep growing in faith, which you'll need, especially if the dream turns out to be formidable. Stay true to your authentic identity. Do not waver. Speak words of faith. Pray. It will happen.

Preparing to Reach Your Potential...

In everything you do and want for your life, ask the Lord to be your confidence...

- In your identity. In your relationships.
- In your dreams. In your goals.
- In your process. In your finances.
- In stewardship. In generosity.
- In your studies. In your future.
- In your decision-making. In your prayers.
- In your words. In your whole life.

God wants to strengthen you to cope confidently and powerfully in this fallen world. Your light was made to shine—brightly. *"In the same way, let your light shine before others, so that they may see your good works and give glory to your Father who is in heaven,"* (Matthew 5:16, ESV).

May your identity be sure and sure-footed. Disciplined and faithful. Steadfast and true in every promise.

The Lord has exciting plans to bless others through you. Christ in you really is the hope of glory. Let Him live through Christ-confident you.

Acknowledgments and Thanks

To the Lord, thank you, Father, for the gift of words: written, spoken, and prayed. I praise you for allowing this book, the passion of my heart, to be published.

To *my Guy*, for inspiring the world with these seven powerful principles of godly success. May *Wealth Confident* be life-changing for everyone who reads it. Thank you for the constancy of your love and the fervor of your devotion for over thirty-two years. How blessed am I that we share one life. Time passes too quickly when you're with the one you love.

To my publisher, Victoria Duerstock, Michelle Medlock Adams, and all the editors, designers, and team at End Game Press, I'm proud and thankful my publisher is you. Thank you for creating gorgeous books that add joy and delight to every reader's experience.

To the great Lori Roeleveld, my writing and publishing coach, thanks again for continuing to steer, shepherd, and save me from many missteps. The indescribable depth of your knowledge and wisdom, the height of your holiness and integrity, and the length of your publishing experience are the winning combination every author needs to reach their finish line.

To my Page 33 writer's critique group, Lori, Jean, Julie, Jeannie, and Lisa, each of you has grown so dear to me. As award-winning, multi-published writers, you inspire me with your unwavering passion for the written word and your holiness as women of God. Thank you for critiquing much of this book and for your unending prayers and godly counsel over my every step.

To the incomparable Eva Marie Everson and Taryn Souders of Word Weavers International, I thank you once again for your tireless efforts to create and sustain the Florida Christian Writers Conference, which gave me the opportunity to connect—and the courage to persevere, now with book number two! This would not have happened without FCWC.

To *"little Vanessa"* Delgado, for over twenty years of loving and faithful assistance. Your friendship and support mean the world to me.

To Chase Neeley and David Loy of Leverage Brands, your marketing strategy helped *Wealth Blessed* achieve Amazon's #2 ranking for Christian stewardship. Thank you for your excellence, care, and fierce advocacy on my behalf. Blessed is the author supported by you.

To my beloved family, especially my faithful brother, Robert, you are the epitome of good. I thank God for you. You are an inspiring and generous model of integrity, Mensa brilliance, and unfailing kindness. To my beautiful sister, Bettina, thanks for loyally pretending I'm not boring you when I report my writing progress each day. To my stepdaughter, Beth, you are *the* most thoughtful person I know. Your love and support fill me up inside.

To Dottie Wobb, for your faithful mentoring for thirty years. I can never repay you.

To the one and only RoseAnn Lovell, my beloved Italian-at-heart soul-sister, for creating generous acts of exciting support. Thank you for actively rallying our friendship troops on my behalf, for arranging a joyous book signing event at your party, and for acts of extreme support too numerous to name. I wish I could write like you!

To the brilliant, dedicated, inspiring Laurie Farquhar, although you're much younger, you're like a mother to me. I cherish our decade of meaningful friendship and thank you for your joy in my journey, for your wise counsel, and for offering generous resources to strengthen my path.

To the talented and innovative Robin Joss, my trusted, loved, and much-admired friend, thank you for your faithful prayer support.

To my close friends near and far, I don't have the space to name you, but my heart thanks you for the gift of your friendship, the impact of your prayers, and the godly example of your love. I pray for you daily, and I love you dearly. Thank you for your gracious patience as I work through my tight schedule to fulfill my calling and mission.

A special call-out to Larry and Marge Henize, whose celebration and support of my work make you feel more like family than friends, and to Diane Klumb, whose intelligence and generosity of spirit make her beloved not just in her community but in my heart.

Elizabeth Brickman, author of *Wealth-Blessed,* which reveals the surprising path to godly financial happiness, is a compassionate expert in the world of financial advising and spiritual wellness. Known as The Caring Advisor, Elizabeth is also a multi-award-winning author whose new series will change readers' lives. As a wealth-confident woman in a profession dominated by male voices, Elizabeth adds a unique perspective that enriches hearts as well as portfolios.

Through her writing, speaking, blogging, and The Caring Advisor podcast, which has reached audiences around the world, Elizabeth offers a distinctive approach to wealth. She helps her audience develop the inner resources of high achievers by tapping into God's power to grow their financial and relational lives with confidence and Christ-centered happiness. Her spiritual insights are rich, loving, and light-hearted.

A former, nationally recognized, award-winning financial advisor and president of her Registered Investment Advisory firm, Elizabeth has a proven track record of success. For twenty-five years, she served private clients from every walk of life in eighteen states. She was regularly quoted in the nationally syndicated financial press and was a periodic guest on Business Financial News radio.

As a Certified Kingdom Advisor, Elizabeth is credentialed to provide financial counsel from a biblical worldview.

Elizabeth offers a much-needed perspective, connecting finance to emotional and spiritual wellness. Her style is engaging, approachable, and fun. She motivates her readers to achieve victorious breakthroughs via innovative, faith-based strategies.

Elizabeth loves her life in sunny South Florida with her beloved husband of over thirty years and her pet orchid, Ophelia.